Happiness

IN A MATERIAL WORLD

The publisher and authors are sincerely grateful to
His Holiness the Fourteenth Dalai Lama and the Office of Tibet,
the Foundation for the Preservation of the Mahayana Tradition,
and the Dalai Lama Committee for their
support and co-operation in the publication of this book.

'Happiness in a Material World: A teaching by the Fourteenth Dalai Lama'
in Chapter Three, translated by Venerable Lhakdor.

The authors dedicate this book to their teachers,
Venerable Traleg Kyabgon Rinpoche
and Venerable Lama Zopa Rinpoche.

Dedicated to my precious teachers and to the memory
of my parents, Kathleen and Wilson Blaikie.
With love and thanks to my children,
my family, my dear friends, and especially Nigel
for his love and support. — AR

Happiness
IN A MATERIAL WORLD

THE DALAI LAMA
IN AUSTRALIA AND NEW ZEALAND

GABRIEL LAFITTE AND ALISON RIBUSH

Lothian
BOOKS

Traditional forms of respect and address for His Holiness and the Sangha have
been shortened or omitted wherever possible, for the benefit of the reader.
The Dalai Lama should be referred to as 'His Holiness'. Whenever mention is
made of an ordained member of the Sangha or an esteemed teacher, please
read 'Venerable' before their name and use this form of address when referring
to them.

The authors have made every effort to ensure the accuracy of the information
contained in this book. However, neither the publisher nor the authors are engaged
in rendering professional advice or services to the individual reader. Readers should
assume responsibility for their own actions, safety and health.

Thomas C. Lothian Pty Ltd
132 Albert Road, South Melbourne, Victoria 3205
www.lothian.com.au

National Library of Australia
Cataloguing-in-Publication data:

Lafitte, Gabriel.
    Happiness in a material world: the Dalai Lama in Australia
    and New Zealand.

    ISBN 0 7344 0426 3.

    1. Bstan-dzin-rgya-mtsho, Dalai Lama XIV, 1935– . 2. Buddhism —
    Australia. 3. Buddhism — New Zealand. 4. Dalai Lamas — Biography.
    5. Buddhism — China — Tibet. I. Ribush, Alison. II. Title.

294.3923092

Series editor: Alison Ribush
Managing Editor: Magnolia Gee
Editors: Frith Luton, Vyvyan Cayley
Text design concept by Kim Roberts Design
Typeset by Caz Brown
Colour reproduction by Digital Imaging Group, Port Melbourne
Printed in Australia by Griffin Press

Contents

Introduction 1

CHAPTER ONE
OPENING THE INNER DOOR:
An introduction to Buddhist practice and principles
15

CHAPTER TWO
ILLUMINATING THE PATH:
The lives of the Fourteenth and Thirteenth Dalai Lamas
and the life story of Atisha
37
The Dalai Lama: his life and work today 40
The Great Thirteenth Dalai Lama (1877–1933) 61
Atisha (982–1054) 72
The Way Forward 79

CHAPTER THREE
HAPPINESS IN A MATERIAL WORLD:
A teaching by the Fourteenth Dalai Lama
83
The Dalai Lama's teachings 86

CHAPTER FOUR
THE PATH TO HAPPINESS:
An explanation of the teachings and initiations
135
The Four Noble Truths 138
Eight Verses of Thought Transformation 147
Atisha's Lamp for the Path to Enlightenment 162
The initiation ceremonies 177
Chenrezig 180
White Tara 183

CHAPTER FIVE
A LAMP FOR THOSE WHO SEEK LIGHT:
Buddhism in Australia and New Zealand
187
Buddhism in Australia 189
Buddhism in New Zealand 215

Glossary 223

Endnotes 233

List of photographs 235

Acknowledgements 236

Recommended reading 237

Buddhist organisations 239

Index 247

Introduction

The 2002 tour of Australia and New Zealand by His Holiness the Fourteenth Dalai Lama is an opportunity to hold up a mirror to ourselves. Great teachers such as the Dalai Lama allow us to see ourselves as we are, without embellishments.

It is not easy to see ourselves dispassionately. Habitually we want the mirror to flatter us, to highlight the best bits and edit out any unflattering aspects. Often, we are too preoccupied with how we look, how we come across and how we are doing. We don't accept ourselves as we are, which makes it hard to change for the better. It takes a special sort of friend to be a mirror, neither distorting our faults nor exaggerating our accomplishments, nor giving us a running commentary of our lives. It is difficult to find a friend who will do that.

People who have spent time in the presence of the great lamas of Tibet quickly experience a sense that the lamas truly know them, with complete acceptance. This seems to happen immediately, quietly and naturally, as though they are in the presence of intimate friends they have come to know over a long time. The lamas accept us better than we accept ourselves, unconditionally, without reservations. It's uncanny. The most revered of these Buddhist teachers is the Dalai Lama, and his visit to Australia and New Zealand in 2002 is a special occasion.

It is often said that the great lamas of Tibet fulfil the wishes of sentient beings. It is said that they are attuned to the needs of all mind-possessors. In our modern material world such claims sound extraordinary, but we all want to be happy, it is what we have most deeply in common. Each person's desire for happiness is in no way exceptional, it is what makes us all equal.

The material world presents us with endless choices. We are concerned about what creates the right look or makes the right statement. We are encouraged to make an individual statement, to stand out from the crowd and express an essential self, but sometimes we experience disappointment when what we invest in doesn't quite live up to our expectations. We become wary of the claim that someone or something can bring us greater happiness.

Tenzin Gyatso, the Buddhist monk we call 'Dalai Lama', can help each of us to become more fully ourselves. He reminds us of what we all have in common. It's basic — sometimes so basic that we overlook it. We live, breathe, eat, walk; and take this for granted. We have long forgotten to marvel and be thankful for the simple things.

The Dalai Lama helps us to make a fresh start. Rather than worrying about our individuality, we can relax into accepting that we are pretty ordinary. This may sound like an anti-climax, but it is a relief. It is an invitation to relax and recognise that our need to work for our happiness should not be somehow privileged ahead of the needs of others. As the Dalai Lama often reminds us, we are all the same in this way. Once we stop privileging our needs, putting ourselves on centre stage, we can relax and let others into our world, experiencing them as they are and sharing what we have in common rather than focusing on our differences.

We have endless choices. We choose to live in cities where in the classroom, at the office, on the dance floor, we can endlessly classify people into who is and isn't the 'right type'. We behave as though life is a rehearsal for a performance. It's exhausting. We hold onto so much — opinions, ideas, fantasies, habits.

The Dalai Lama has an alternative. It begins by relaxing, using relaxation as the heart of a secret method. When we relax, life is no longer so serious. There is more room, more space to let things happen, rather than maintaining the fiction that we are the authors of everything. To relax is to slow down, to find time to meditate and experience ourselves as we are. To relax is to let problems dissolve of their own accord, like clouds disappearing from the sky. When we relax, we are more receptive, appreciative, flexible and open to others and their needs. Relaxation is a beginning.

Relaxation is also a Buddhist method of meditation. Meditation is understood differently in other traditions. Buddhists don't particularly aim just to manufacture calmness and peacefulness. Buddhist meditation isn't a matter of trying to create this or that. It's a basic relaxation into experiencing what is and accepting whatever arises, as it is, without judging it. Meditation takes the mirror offered by the presence of the teacher and puts it in our own hands so that we experience our mind. We sit with the confusions, anxieties, hopes, fears and rolling emotions as they arise, aware of them moment by moment, without censoring them or becoming engrossed in them. To do this requires some alertness and balance, and a sense of humour.

With patience, meditation leads somewhere. Meditation is a process of familiarisation in which we come home to ourselves, make friends with ourselves as we are and grow in confidence. We awaken to things as they are, rather than living as victims of hope and fear, pushed and pulled by our ideas of what and who we should be. Change begins with relaxation and acceptance. With relaxation we no longer force ourselves to change any of the countless harmful habits that keep us in a cycle of dissatisfaction, because force is counter-productive, whether applied to ourselves or to others.

When we are relaxed and confident we see how ridiculous it is to expect to be perfect, or to be different, or to try to make a statement in the world. We wake up and discover we are ordinary and that each moment is actually quite extraordinary, if only we are paying attention fully and are fully alive. We no longer live as if preparing to live, but recognise that life is now.

When we live in the moment, we are ready to help others, not just as an aspiration but as a capability. We can only help others if we are open to them, and can dissolve the distance between us. We help ourselves and we help others. Nurturing self-esteem, we discover a calm appreciation of ourselves as we are, which is the basis for discovering others as they are.

A mirror will not tell us how to live our life, but lets us see ourselves as we are, giving us a realistic basis for change and growth and enabling us to shed old habits that have us going around in circles. From a Buddhist point of view, we have an innate ability to awaken from our habitual routines. Awakening begins when we see, taste, experience and accept ourselves as we actually are. That is a solid, tangible basis for growth and change, rather than straining to live up to an ideal. Once we have subdued the mind we can start to train it.

The Dalai Lama's aim is to help us gain confidence in being who we are, as a grounded basis for developing our capacities for kindness, compassion and insight into the human condition.

The Dalai Lama has a wonderful sense of humour. Sometimes, when he is asked to comment on a burning moral issue, he responds with compassionate humour. People want guidance and rules, only to resent them, and the Dalai Lama isn't in the business of complicating our lives with rules, packaging the world into neat bundles of right and wrong. He invites us to open our eyes, see ourselves anew, soften our hearts to others, and allow our compassion to naturally arise and blossom. He is likely to unsettle our categories, shift our perspective and encourage us to ask ourselves why we find life problematic. He might even go so far as to suggest that we make our lives problematic by assuming we have problems. If we hold onto the idea that we have problems, we are forever seeking solutions, treating life as an exercise in management.

If we see the Dalai Lama as a person who has awoken, who trusts himself and has experienced the wide range of mind trainings encompassed by Buddhism, we begin to trust him as someone who is without illusions or self-deception and we take a step towards our own greater self-confidence.

The Dalai Lama fulfils the wishes of all beings by being himself. He reminds us that neither he nor the historic Shakyamuni Buddha had any miraculous means of delivering us from our own illusions. If they did have such magic short-cuts we would all be enlightened by now, for our liberation is the intention of all Buddhas, past, present and future. But, as the Buddha said, each of us must take responsibility for our own liberation. No one can do it for us.

The Buddha has offered us a set of tools to create our own happiness and, by being happy, bring happiness to others. Tools are not to be worshipped but to be used, for as long as they are actually useful. In a classic Buddhist image, the teach-ings of the Buddha are a boat that enables us to get across the raging river of life, a river too turbulent to swim alone. The teachings of the Buddha, and those who had the confidence to do as the historic Buddha did, offer us many ways of getting on with life here and now.

The presence of the Dalai Lama brings the teachings to life. While it can be hard to relate to a text, it is natural to relate to a living example of the teachings. This is another reason why the Dalai Lama and other great teachers are so precious. They fulfil the needs of people by keeping it simple, reminding us of what really matters.

To be in the presence of the Dalai Lama is to be in the presence of all enlightened teachers and the many generations of practitioners who awoke to discover the empty, fluid and accommodating nature of mind. This is the secret. What we hang onto is insubstantial, and is produced by specific circumstances, causes and conditions. We can let go because there isn't actually anything solid or absolute to hang onto, and hanging on only shuts us off, distancing us from reality.

It's inspiring to be around someone who meditates daily on the insubstantiality — *shunyata* — of everything we'd like to believe is solid. They have an ability to empathise with others.

To realise that everything in the world is insubstantial, contingent and dependent on circumstances is to realise that the same is true of the self. There is no essential self to find, no real 'me'. We are free to be whatever we choose to be. We are free to take up whatever role suits the situation or simply be an ensemble of roles. To discover that the self is an ever-changing construct is to be free to relax and take things as they come.

There are many Buddhist practices to create happiness, but the most profound is insight into shunyata (emptiness). When we realise there is nothing to hang onto and there is no unchanging essential self, we are radically free. This is transcendent knowledge, an insight into the way everything exists. In theory it may make sense that nothing exists independently, but only when it becomes an experienced reality does it set us free.

To be in the presence of the Dalai Lama is to be in an ongoing relationship. The Dalai Lama invites us to celebrate that relationship by taking refuge. If we take refuge or one of the initiations he offers, we openly acknowledge our relationship, not just with the Dalai Lama but with ourselves and our ability for spiritual growth. We take or renew our vows as a way of making a commitment to our training in insight and compassion. We can take a vow or initiation as a way of becoming part of a family of practitioners, of fellow 'refugees' who find common refuge in something that is trustworthy.

We do not need to externalise the deities whose initiations are offered for us to take on this tour (Chenrezig and Tara) as they are qualities we all possess, they are representations of the finest of human capacities. Chenrezig embodies the human capability for compassion, which allows us to encounter others as they are, with a sense of appreciation and responsiveness. In meditation we see Chenrezig before us, become one with Chenrezig and dissolve the visualisation back into the creative mind. And we can recognise the Dalai Lama, the 'precious protector' as Tibetans call him, as an embodiment of Chenrezig.

In meditation we can also invoke the presence of White Tara. She is the embodied form of clear-sighted wisdom and the transcendent knowledge of how reality exists, combined with heartfelt compassion. She is penetrating insight into the nature of all that arises, all phenomena internal and external, subjective and objective. She is the original perfect purity of mind, uncluttered by the stuff we usually think is important.

When we look closely at Buddhism we discover there is no dogma or doctrine we have to sign onto in order to be a Buddhist. There isn't a package of beliefs that makes us Buddhist. The Dalai Lama emphasises again and again that what matters is not a label or a lifestyle statement, but whether you live authentically, with a genuine appreciation of yourself and those around you.

A visit by a Dalai Lama is brief. He is in demand all over the world, and after four decades in exile is still a refugee working for his people. He offers us tools to discover happiness, and this book offers practical ways to maintain your relationship with the Dalai Lama, whether he is physically present or not.

In Australia and New Zealand there are now hundreds of Buddhist temples, presenting Buddhism in all its diversity. There is a growing maturity of Buddhism in Australia and

New Zealand, as practice deepens under the guidance of trained, fully qualified teachers from traditional lineages. Direct connection to a lineage is our guarantee of quality, of accessing one of the world's great religious traditions with confidence in its authenticity.

Buddhism in Australia goes back to the gold fields of the 1850s. The New Gold Mountain temple in Bendigo, Victoria — usually called the Joss House — has a monk with his begging bowl at the entrance to this day. In the Canterbury Plains gold field of New Zealand's South Island archaeologists have recovered Buddha images from the diggings. Both countries have welcomed settlers and refugees from Buddhist countries, who established temples reflecting the national styles and aesthetics of almost every country in Asia. Today there is no city of more than 100,000 people without a Buddhist community and resident teacher. Many smaller centres are also well established, especially in beautiful rural areas suited to meditation retreats.

Buddhist societies of pakeha and Anglo-Australians were founded in the 1930s, attracting strong personalities drawn to a different path. These pioneers gradually found ways of inviting monks and nuns, often from Sri Lanka or Thailand, to visit and teach meditation. The first resident monk for the Buddhist Society of Victoria arrived in 1979. His students weren't always sure how to look after him, and after a few months he gently said, 'It is easy to buy an elephant but the difficulty is in keeping it.'

Within Tibetan Buddhism alone there are now dozens of communities, from Cairns to Perth, Whangarei to Dunedin, with resident teachers fully qualified in traditional Tibetan meditative practice and realisation. We now have annual Buddhist Summer Schools showcasing all traditions together, performances and exhibitions by Buddhist artists and musicians, regular Buddhism and psychotherapy workshops, interfaith dialogues and engaged Buddhist activism for peace and reconciliation. There are many Buddhist social-welfare programmes, including counselling of prisoners, guidance and hospices for the dying and their families. There are retreat centres for intensive life-transforming practice. There is a steady stream of visiting teachers in addition to those *geshes* and *lamas* who chose to live among us as much as twenty-five years ago. And as Buddhism matures, community grows.

This book provides a general introduction to Buddhism, the Dalai Lama and the teachings and initiations he will give in Australia and New Zealand in 2002. By reading about the person Tibetans simply call 'The Presence' or 'Kundun', you may find yourself better prepared for his teachings. If you read it after your encounter with him, you may find it clarifies how and why so many people from different backgrounds respond so fully to him. And if you do not meet him, this book gives you something of the flavour of his life, his practical advice about handling the decisions of modern life, and an insight into the timeless universal teachings of Buddhism, designed for people everywhere.

May all beings be happy.

CHAPTER ONE

OPENING THE INNER DOOR:
An introduction to Buddhist practice and principles

Buddhism is a modern word, which has no equivalent in Tibetan. The people we would call Buddhist 'meditators' or 'practitioners', Tibetans call those who 'go within' and change their minds by doing so. To go within is to discover the human mind and its capabilities. Through meditation, habitual restrictions are overcome, the inner door opens and compassion awakens.

But this does not entail signing up for a package of beliefs based on divine authority or the revelation granted exclusively to the founder. Because it is not based on one person or a single moment in history, Buddhist practice is renewed by all practitioners who awaken, and they in turn renew others.

As the Dalai Lama explains in Chapter Three, the Buddha is not a divinity but an ordinary human being who awoke to the true nature of things. What the historic Buddha did, we can do. To awaken is to be free of illusion. It is a falling away of delusional habits rather than the creation of something new. The Buddha ceased to be a victim of circumstances, swayed by events of the outside world or torn by conflicting emotions. He discovered the human mind's full creativity, and it was blissful.

He had gained insight into the nature of reality beyond concepts, but had to use a conceptual framework to point the way for others to discover that truth for themselves. Some of the words and concepts we associate with Buddhism are quite familiar words even in Western societies.

Meditation

First, let us consider what the Buddha taught as the heart of Buddhism: meditation. Meditation is an essential and powerful tool for discovering the nature of the mind and the phenomenal world, not only in formal meditation practice but also in ordinary situations. Training the mind to settle, to see beyond the surface of events and to steadily experience itself is a balancing act. It can take some getting used to. Force of habit drags the mind off centre, plunging us into stories of who we are and where others fit in, and we quickly lose whatever perspective we may have had. To sit on a meditation cushion is to sit with whatever arises, neither censoring it nor getting lost in it. Meditation takes practice. It is not a magical short-cut to a blank or peaceful, serene mind. Instead, meditators practise moment-to-moment awareness, whether of the physical feelings in the body, sensations from outside — a noise, the scent of a flower — or emotions and thoughts arising from within. These can't be, and aren't shut out or denied, for that only makes their return stronger. Nor are they entertained, invited to take over and occupy our entire conscious mind. They are allowed to arise and disappear of their own accord. Tides of emotion, sharp and dull thoughts, fantasies, memories, obsessions — all sorts of things come up. The trick is to stay mindful.

When we aren't trying to meditate, we discover the ability to watch the dynamic movement of the mind in a gentle yet alert way, without getting pulled into a storyline or shutting out what seems unattractive. This is being mindful moment by moment of what is happening. It is the foundation of Buddhist mind training.

What people notice when they first sit with no distractions is that the mind generates a lot. The amount of thoughts that arise can even be alarming. It is humbling to discover that, far from the mind controlling everything, the mind itself seems somewhat random and almost out of control. To notice this is a first step. Meditation is a chance to meet ourselves as we haven't before, simply and directly, with perspective and without falling into complex storylines and judgements of what is right and wrong. To just be aware of our thoughts but not distracted by them is at first quite difficult.

Meditation means becoming familiar with our own mind and with what is. The more we know ourselves as we are, the less inclined we are to trip off into a fantasy of who we think we should be or could be. To become familiar is to loosen up and relax, to become more accommodating and more responsive to others. To be responsive without attachment or projection is to be compassionate.

People who meditate say that through meditation you come home to yourself, be yourself, relax, and meet the mind not only at its surface of thoughts and events but also in its more creative depths. We also examine aspects of Buddhism, such as karma, rebirth, the Three Jewels and nirvana.

Karma

Historically, Buddhism originated in India and evolved in energetic dialogue with Hinduism. Many key terms are shared, but have quite different meanings, which has led to some confusion. What Buddhists mean by karma is not a fixed destiny that can only be fatalistically accepted. From a Buddhist point of view, karma is simply the working of cause and effect; a reminder to be mindful of the consequences of whatever we do and the motives behind our actions. These actions encompass those of our body, speech and mind. Who we are today is the consequence of decisions we made in the past. This means that we have a choice about who we become tomorrow. Even if in the past we have developed habits that narrow our lives and constrict the future, we are free to make the future. We can choose to remain a prisoner of habit or develop insight and effective compassion.

Karma does not work simply or predictably in our complex world, yet in the long run it works surely and unmistakeably. The causes and conditions that give rise to situations are so interdependent that no one can be certain about when the consequences of their actions will bear fruit. But skilful actions motivated by unconditional compassion are certain to bear wholesome fruit; while ill-intentioned actions designed to exclude or hurt eventually bring bad results. That's the logic of karma. It's common sense, not a matter of divine intervention. It can be relied on, not as a doctrine but as practical inspiration for life.

Rebirth

Rebirth is not a doctrine but an observation that life doesn't appear from nothing, and that each of us is born with a personality, predispositions and inclinations. Perhaps genetics can explain how three or four children of the same mother and father display quite different temperaments from birth, or perhaps we have had previous existences.

A belief in rebirth should not be a soft option: 'It doesn't really matter if I don't get my act together in this life, because there's always a next life in which to do it.' From a Buddhist point of view, that's sentimental, naïve and a denial of how we live now. If we don't have our act together we suffer now. To rely on rebirth is just to prolong the mess.

So what is it that goes from one life to another? Unlike Hindus who believe in a substantial eternal soul, Buddhists think that only the most ingrained habits of mind that constitute our core definition of 'self' can be transmitted. Only these subconscious imprints on the mind are strong enough to persist, to survive the loss of the body at death. The positive habits result in fortunate circumstances, such as living in a peaceful place with good material resources, intelligence and other advantages; the negative habits perpetuate our confusion and dissatisfaction. The prospect of taking birth in some shape or form less fortunate than being born human is hardly reassuring. Rebirth has a practical value as a reminder that we need to get our act together in this lifetime. The prospect of having to repeat the same mistakes is not attractive. A belief in rebirth helps to motivate meditation practice.

Although nearly all of us are prisoners of habit, there are some among us who have fully awoken to the nature of mind, and have let go of everything that seems solid. They are not only happy but capable of showing others the way. These few are the great lamas, the greatest of whom is the Dalai Lama. He in turn takes inspiration from the life of Atisha. Such people need not take rebirth compulsively, driven by habit, because they are no longer enslaved by self-inflicted routines but live freely, open to all that arises. These capable Buddhist teachers have fully realised the choices open to them, and could choose to cease taking rebirth. If they were thinking only of themselves, perhaps they would end the cycle of rebirth. But they aren't just thinking of themselves. Their perspective is all-inclusive, and their motivation is to do whatever is possible to help others awaken to the human condition. So these few great lamas take rebirth voluntarily, for the sake of others. They ensure there is always an incarnate presence of wisdom and guidance for those who remain habitually locked into hope and fear, expectation and disappointment.

Nirvana and samsara

Nirvana is a word and a concept that's familiar. Yet its Buddhist meaning is unexpected. It could mean some sort of heaven, an ultimate destination in which all our problems are over, the final point on the path of spiritual growth. Yet as a destination it is also very earthly and uncannily familiar. Nirvana is the freedom from delusions, suffering and karma.

Conventionally, the ordinary world of confusion, anxiety, unpredictability and dissatisfaction is called *samsara*. Samsara can be alluring but often we seem to be going round in circles, making little progress. If we take the spiritual journey, undertake the mind training and discover what it is to be fully human, we can appreciate what is remarkable about each moment, as we are no longer driven by habit.

We may need many spiritual practices, and considerable guidance, in order to awaken fully, to truly change the mind, to undo our compulsions and conditioning. But change we can. We take the Buddhist paths of purification, concentration, relaxation, insight and awakening. Samsara and nirvana can be two inseparable ways of looking at the same situation.

Training the mind

The Buddha has given us a collection of tools. The classic Buddhist image is of the Dharma (Buddhist teachings) as a raft. We stand on the bank of the turbulent river of life, knowing we must cross to the far side. If we plunge in we risk being swept away. But a raft can carry us safely across. Having safely crossed, do we then carry it with us wherever we go? No.

Buddhism is a useful tool, but it is not an object of worship in its own right.

We need rafts of all shapes and sizes to regain our freedom and deal with the trickster — the mind. The self-centred mind that puts us at the epicentre of our world claims to be the real, true, essential 'me'; the author of our lives and protector of our interests. Until now we have believed its claims. It is forever telling us that happiness is almost within our grasp, and we followed wherever it led us. Now Buddhism tells us that it is a false friend, not to be relied on, more a cause of frustration and disappointment than a source of abiding happiness.

This restless ego-mind might even bring us to see the Dalai Lama, or try meditation in the hope that this is the technique we need. Often when we attend a teaching or sit on a cushion, ego takes the credit. Far from yielding, ego expands its territory. Some lamas call this 'spiritual materialism'. It turns Buddhism into another lifestyle statement — a way of letting the world know that we are attuned.

When we sit, the storyline of the contrived self starts to fall apart. We like to think of ourselves as practical, in control and on top of things; but when we sit on the meditation cushion, what arises is a jumble of powerful emotions and random thoughts. There seems to be no 'I' at the wheel. Sometimes the same obsessive patterns come back again and again. At times it is not the case that 'I' think 'my' thoughts, it's more that the thoughts think 'me'. This is definitely humbling.

Buddhism reminds us to be gentle and patient in these first moments of awakening. We just sit with whatever arises, noticing it, tasting the flavour of all emotions, thoughts and sensations, without turning away or plunging into the drama. It's tricky to maintain a balance, but in all things Buddhism is a middle way between the extremes of denial and fascination. We learn how the mind can watch the mind, and is the only tool for doing so.

Buddhist practice opens a space in which we can relax and discover the full range of Buddhist methods for awakening from the self-hypnosis we have set up. But our self-centredness isn't done with us yet. When we have a good session of meditation, ego-mind moves in silently to take the credit. 'You're making progress,' it says. It creates attachment to what happened, triggering a craving for more, a desire to savour a moment that is already the past, rather than moving on in the present. Or if we have a bad session, the mind is jumbled, the body twitchy, emotions rise in a torrent and agitation takes over. 'You can't meditate,' ego-mind says. 'You aren't making any progress.' We get depressed, or vow to try harder to get it right.

We may decide to fight the obstacles, or walk away and say Buddhism is useless. But all these responses are the old

trickster claiming to be author, judge and jury of all that con-
stitutes 'me'. When we judge, we are again stuck in the past
and in expectations of the future, rather than quietly taking
each moment as it comes. We again elaborate a storyline to
explain what it all means, and all this does is complicate what
is simple.

Buddhism is useful, because it offers us an extraordinary
range of ways to deal with the ego. Some methods are blunt,
such as direct antidotes for obstacles. The *Eight Verses of Thought
Transformation* offers many such antidotes. Other methods are
less forceful and rely more on patience and trust in oneself.
When the anxious ego-driven questions arise, a relaxed response
is to recollect that it doesn't matter, just keep going, just keep
breathing and maintaining mindfulness. To be a modern person
is to think too much. The solution is to simply acknowledge
everything arising as a thought, and let it be.

From a Buddhist point of view the self has its uses. It organises
the practical realities of daily life. But when it claims to be in
control and everything has to pass through its filter of likes and
dislikes, it is no longer a servant. It is on the loose and we are
enslaved. The Dalai Lama says that people invent ideologies in
the search for a happy society, but all too often they end up

becoming its slaves. The same goes for the personal ideology of the self.

Buddhism deals with the demands of the self through a thousand methods, which are tailored to skilfully address obsessive self-concern. We constantly compare ourselves to other meditators. We sit on a cushion and fantasise about the wonderful things we will do as Buddhists. We study texts and philosophical systems and feel we have truly understood them, only to find at the next crisis in our life that we are as helpless as ever. We master ritual practices in obsessive detail but somehow miss the point of softening and opening our hearts. We attend a teaching by the Dalai Lama and feel at peace with ourselves and the world, but forget the next day to maintain our meditation practice. These are among the myriad ways old habits reassert their control over us.

When we practise Buddhism, we do it obsessively. That's inevitable. We bring to our practice all the habits, strategies, routines and self-definitions we have built up over a lifetime — or perhaps many lifetimes. From a Buddhist point of view that's not a problem, because Buddhism exists for all of us stuck in our self-defeating routines. There's no shame in acknowledging it. It can even be a relief.

Can we really change this neurotic mind of ours into a mind that is happy and engaged with the world, a mind that

illuminates each moment with clarity and freshness? The Dalai
Lama says we can. He says:

'The thing that we call "mind" is quite peculiar. Sometimes
it is very stubborn and very difficult to change. But with continuous
effort and with conviction based on reason, our minds are sometimes
quite honest. When we really feel that there is some need to change,
then our minds can change. Wishing and praying alone will not
transform your mind, but with conviction and reason, you can transform your mind.'[1]

Buddhism has a variety of methods. Tibetan Buddhism
emphasises the practical value of a connection with a living
teacher, as someone who has already travelled the path, someone trustworthy and compassionate yet unsentimental. These
are the qualities of the lamas. They know which practice best
suits which practitioner at any particular time; they accept us
without judgements.

The relationship with a teacher is not a surrender to
someone with power. Buddhist teachers strongly suggest that
blind faith is the wrong approach, and that an initial scepticism
is healthy. Students need to investigate their teachers. The best
situation is one in which a real bond grows naturally through
the opportunity to see for oneself whether the teachings are
a meaningful, lived reality in the teacher's life. Atisha braved
typhoons to find a teacher who could help him awaken fully.

The Three Jewels

Buddhists take refuge in the historic Buddha, in his teachings and in the community of practitioners past and present. These are commonly known by their Sanskrit names: Buddha, Dharma and Sangha. They are also referred to as the Three Jewels or Triple Gem. They inspire us to take to the path.

The historic Buddha is not a physical presence any more, and his teachings may or may not come to life as we read them, but the Sangha are available to us as a support. It is ideal to have a living person who embodies the qualities of the historic Buddha, who lives the teachings and who is a sure guide and spiritual friend on the path, having already traversed it. This is why Tibetans accord a special place to the lamas, a word that means 'none higher'.

As we develop confidence in our teachers through their guidance, we gain greater confidence in ourselves. We also notice the great confidence and reverence they have for their teachers. Tibetan Buddhism is organised in lineages, Atisha being the founder of a major lineage. These are sometimes called 'schools', as though there are major philosophical differences between them, but there aren't. Lineages trace back the intimate friendships of student and teacher. An entire lineage tree can be visualised as part of the process of joining a family that can be trusted. The four lineages of Tibetan Buddhism in order of their historic appearance are the *Nyingma, Kagyu, Sakya* and *Gelugpa.*

The intimate connection between teacher and student can flourish through the formal ritual of initiation and empowerment, the entry into a new practice. To request an empowerment for a specific Buddhist practice honours the teacher and the entire lineage. It shows that the student is strongly motivated. The ceremony seals our commitment and gives us strength to persist when boredom sets in. When a teacher gives an empowerment, he or she is giving permission for us to practise. This can purify the mind, foster mental stability, concentration, generosity, compassion and other spiritual qualities.

It's up to us to do the practice to transform our mind. The initiation alone may not transform us, but it can be deeply inspiring if we are receptive. It can be a blessing, and an act of belonging and inclusiveness among those who 'go within'. In a way, we bless ourselves. Buddhism is a reminder that it's good to be alive, to be able to take the next breath.

The Buddhist tradition continues to evolve as each generation of insightful practitioners adds to the rich variety of techniques. Each new generation of enlightened teachers finds new ways to spark the imagination, commitment and hard work needed for the natural mind to shine through the clouded habitual mind. The repertoire of paths is amazing.

Dancers can discover ultimate reality through the slow, meditative dance forms of Buddhism. Artists can connect with the visual language of enlightenment of Buddhist sculptors and painters, both classical and contemporary, including recent Buddhist artists such as Ian Fairweather, Ross Moore, Karma Phuntsok, Kerryl Shirley and Lama Karma Samten. Computer enthusiasts can find Buddhism presented as elegant nested systems of tenets and syllogisms. Open-hearted people find teachers who emphasise devotion, loving kindness and compassion from the start. There are repetitive practices that allow purification to arise. Poets find the hazy moon of enlightenment evoked by thousands of Buddhist poets, from Atisha and Milarepa a thousand years ago to Australian contemporaries such as Robert Gray and Harold Stewart. This does not mean that Buddhism has lost sight of its original purity. The goal of awakening to the insubstantiality of all phenomena of the material world and the mind and to be freed by this insight, remains the same. But the skilful means of pointing to what is beyond continue.

Some people say Buddhism is now fashionable, so it must be suspect. This is glib and cynical. The reasons some people turn to Buddhism may be initially superficial, but Buddhists don't have a problem with that. When people start to meditate they soon discover that Buddhism isn't a lifestyle statement and it can't be reduced to a fashion. Where people begin isn't where they end up. Buddhist practice challenges us to get real and be genuine. It holds up a mirror that shows us when we're faking it. The great lamas welcome everyone to Buddhism, because they treat everyone equally. Everyone has a chance to get beyond what motivated their first step.

In Buddhism there is a deep confidence that people have a natural capacity to grow and awaken, to go beyond their starting point. To deny our capacity for growth is pessimistic.

Buddhism is a true awakening, in the deepest sense. Yet if we take the path, elude the traps set by a grasping ego-mind and awaken, it's not a Buddhist awakening. The point of Buddhist practice is not to become a Buddhist, but to be more fully and authentically at home in the world. We discover that this material world is quite manageable, once the self is in proportion. We are utterly free and ordinary. The foibles of others are no longer something we recoil from. We accept others as they are, wholeheartedly and unconditionally. Compassion arises in us for all beings still seeking happiness. It arises in an awakened mind along with the skills needed to communicate effectively and help others awaken too.

During his Melbourne visit in 1992, the Dalai Lama said compassion is not only at the heart of Buddhism, but all religious traditions:

'The essential teaching of all the religious traditions is compassion, or human affection. Without human affection, even religious beliefs can become destructive. Thus, the essence, even in religion, is a good heart. I consider human affection, or compassion, to be the universal religion.

'Whether a believer or a non-believer, everyone needs human affection and compassion, because compassion gives us inner strength, hope and mental peace.

'If we are in a good mood when we get up in the morning, if there is a warm-hearted feeling within, automatically our inner door is opened for that day. Even should an unfriendly person happen along, we would not experience much disturbance and may even manage to say something nice to that person. But on a day when our mood is less positive and we are feeling irritated, automatically our inner door closes. As a result, even if we encounter our best friend, we feel uncomfortable and strained. These instances show how our inner attitude makes a great difference in our daily experiences. Therefore, in order to create a pleasant atmosphere within ourselves, within our families, within our communities, we have to realise that the ultimate source of that pleasant atmosphere is within the individual, within each of us — a good heart, human compassion, love.

'Without human friendship, without the human smile, our life becomes miserable. The lonely feeling becomes unbearable. It is a natural law — that is to say, according to natural law we depend on others to live. If our attitude toward fellow human beings, on whom we depend, becomes hostile, how can we hope to attain peace of mind or a happy life?'[2]

CHAPTER TWO

ILLUMINATING THE PATH:
The lives of the Fourteenth and
Thirteenth Dalai Lamas
and the life story of Atisha

In this chapter we tell the stories of three men, the current Fourteenth Dalai Lama, his predecessor, the Great Thirteenth Dalai Lama, and Atisha, author of *The Lamp for the Path to Enlightenment.*

The Fourteenth Dalai Lama left Tibet in 1959, forced into exile by the occupation of his country. Many Tibetans fled with him, and established new lives in Asia or in the West. This allowed the wisdom of Tibet to spread and flourish in the rest of the world. Ancient texts, knowledge and experience, teachings and oral transmissions handed down through the centuries have been introduced to us by the Dalai Lama, illuminating the way for us to follow.

The Great Thirteenth Dalai Lama, after also spending some time in exile, returned to Tibet. He reformed his country, revived Buddhism, encouraged the training of Buddhist scholars, fostered the sacred arts, and he was to begin the process of modernisation.

Atisha was an eleventh-century Indian monk who, after travelling to Sumatra, was invited to Tibet by the King of Western Tibet. The practice of Buddhism was in disarray in Tibet, and Atisha, wishing to help all beings, agreed to make the journey and re-establish the teachings. He was responsible for a renaissance, the 'second spread' of teachings, which led to the foundation of the three new schools of Buddhism. His famous text *The Lamp for the Path to Enlightenment* was written for Tibetans to light the way and inspire them to practise.

The Dalai Lama: his life and work today

Tenzin Gyatso, His Holiness the Dalai Lama of Tibet, was born in 1935 in a small village called Taktser, 'the Roaring Tiger', in the far north-east of Tibet. Like many of the Dalai Lamas before him, he was born into an ordinary family of smallholder farmers. He was formally recognised at the age of two, after a delegation of lamas from Lhasa identified him.

His predecessor, the Thirteenth Dalai Lama had left some signs and instructions about where the young reincarnated lama would be found, and after rigorous investigations the child was identified and confirmed as the new leader of the Tibetan people. The young child and his family undertook a three-month journey across the desolate plains until they arrived in Lhasa where government officials and crowds gathered to greet their new Dalai Lama.

The Dalai Lama's first year in Lhasa was spent in the *Norbulingka*, the Jewel Park, a summer palace surrounded by beautiful gardens. Here among the majestic trees, flowers, ponds, and even a private zoo, the young Dalai Lama and his family, adjusted to his new life. He was formally installed as Dalai Lama on the Lion Throne on 22 February 1940, and his full name became Jamphel Ngawang Lobsang Yeshe Tenzin Gyatso. The Dalai Lama took up residence in the Potala palace, and began his monastic education to prepare for when he would assume full temporal and spiritual responsibility for his nation. He completed his *Geshe Lharampa* degree (which is roughly equivalent to a doctorate in Buddhist philosophy) at the age of twenty-four.

Tenzin Gyatso is the latest in a long line of Dalai Lamas, each considered to be the reincarnation of the same being. The Dalai Lama, whose name means Ocean of Wisdom, is the leader of the Tibetan nation and is much loved by all his people.

Every Dalai Lama is believed to be the living embodiment and manifestation of the Buddha of compassion, *Chenrezig*. Chenrezig symbolises altruistic compassion at the highest level and this quality is obvious in the man who refers to himself as 'a simple monk'. The Dalai Lama is now in his mid-sixties, and generally enjoys good health. He has said that if Tibet is still occupied when it is time for him to die, his next reincarnation will be born in exile, in a free country.

The Dalai Lama became the head of the Gelugpa School or lineage of Tibet, one of the four lineages (Nyingma, Kagyu, Sakya and Gelugpa) that have evolved since Buddhism was introduced to Tibet from India. Although he is a supremely devoted adherent of the Gelugpa school, he has a deep commitment to non-sectarianism, and encourages students to listen to or take teachings from qualified teachers of all four schools.

The Dalai Lama's respect for diverse views extends to all religious and spiritual traditions. He has repeatedly expressed his opinion that people should not change or abandon their own religion or cultural heritage. He believes that a multiplicity of faiths is necessary for the wide variety of people on the earth.

In 1950 as China invaded Tibet, the Dalai Lama assumed full responsibility for his country. Despite travelling to Beijing since then to meet with Chinese leaders, he has been unable to secure a peaceful solution for Tibet. After an uprising in the capital, Lhasa, in 1959, which was suppressed by the Chinese army, the Dalai Lama fled to India in a dangerous and exhausting escape over the Himalayas. More than 80,000 refugees made the terrifying and treacherous journey to follow him into exile, and on arrival in India many of them were given political asylum. Many monks and nuns also escaped, and began their exile by re-establishing their monastic communities in India or Nepal.

Today there are more than 120,000 Tibetans living in exile, many in the West. The Dalai Lama is a unifying force; he has remained a source of comfort and inspiration for his people in the most difficult circumstances. He is leader of a cohesive population of Tibetans who have been under threat of genocide, and he guides all Tibetan people in exile.

Since going into exile himself, the Dalai Lama has become a well-recognised and well-respected figure world wide. He is recognised as the supreme teacher of Tibetan Buddhism, and he travels widely, teaching, attending forums, and giving public lectures often to thousands of people. In 2002 he will visit Australia for the fourth time since 1982. He has made many visits to Europe and the United States of America, and has taught in the former Union of Soviet Socialist Republics and Mongolia. He has visited South America, Taiwan and South-East Asia, and is constantly requested to return by those who have been inspired by his presence. The Dalai Lama's official residence is in Dharamsala, an Indian hill-station in the Himalayas, where the Tibetan Government-in-Exile is based. In 1960 the government of India gave land to the Tibetans, who have since established government offices, schools, hospitals and orphanages. Since leaving Tibet, the Dalai Lama has worked to establish a democratic system of government, and has said that he will hand over the political leadership of the government to an elected body.

When the Dalai Lama is home in the Himalayas he lives the life of a Buddhist monk in a small cottage near his offices. He rises early every morning, between 3.00 and 4.00, to meditate and study. In the tradition of all Buddhist monks, he eats simple meals and has a modest way of life. The BBC World Service programme provides much of his information of the world's news and events. During the day he has a busy programme of meetings with his administrative staff and government officials, private audiences with visitors, religious teachings and ceremonies, and he tries to meet all newly arrived refugees from Tibet.

Through the recognition and respect of the international community, over fifty major awards have been conferred on the Dalai Lama. In 1989 he was awarded the Nobel Peace Prize in Oslo. The Nobel Peace Prize committee emphasised the fact that in his struggle for the liberation of Tibet he consistently opposed the use of violence, instead advocating peaceful solutions based upon tolerance and mutual respect to conserve the historical and cultural heritage of his people. The Dalai Lama accepted the prize on behalf of the oppressed everywhere, all those who struggle for freedom and work for world peace, and the people of Tibet. He has also received the Raoul Wallenberg Human Rights Award, an Honorary Doctorate of Laws from the University of Melbourne, the Earth Prize from the United Nations Environmental Programme, and the Alexandra Tolstoy Humanitarian Award.

The principles of interdependency and the desire to cause no harm to any living being are the foundations of Tibetan Buddhism. All Tibetans understand and respect the environment, and over the centuries have taken great care not to exploit the natural world. This is a direct result of religious ideals, which propose that people live in harmony with everything around them. For centuries the now harsh Tibetan landscape was managed as a perfect eco-system, brimming with wildlife, forests and grasslands. Early visitors to Tibet from the West describe vast areas of natural beauty, surrounded by the highest mountains on earth, covered in snow. Herds of gazelles, yaks and wild ponies roamed freely.

The Dalai Lama has continued to promote the environmental ideals of Tibetans, attending ecological conferences and presenting papers. In his Nobel Peace Prize address, he proposed:

'It is my dream that the entire Tibetan plateau should become a free refuge where humanity and nature can live in peace and in harmonious balance. It would be a place where people from all over the world could come to seek the true meaning of peace within themselves, away from the tensions and pressures of much of the rest of the world. Tibet could indeed become the creative centre for the promotion and development of peace.'[1]

There are several charities and welfare organisations dedicated to assisting Tibetans. One such organisation is the Tibet House Trust, inaugurated by the Dalai Lama in 1994. The purpose is to preserve the Tibetan culture and identity, and to rehabilitate Tibetan refugees. The Trust maintains reception centres for refugees who continue to flee their country; as well as hospitals, schools, monasteries and nunneries, training workshops, and cultural education programmes. Tibetans in exile have adapted well to their new circumstances, and their religion and culture have flourished outside their country. The Dalai Lama is patron of many trusts, and any money that is presented to him is given directly to these trusts, to aid and relieve the sufferings of the Tibetan people.

The Dalai Lama immediately responds to the desperate situations people experience, whatever their background. In January 2001, on hearing of the earthquake in Gujarat, India, he asked the crowd of around 4000 people attending an annual Dharma celebration to join him in reciting the mantra of compassion, to benefit victims of the disaster. He then made a personal contribution of funds, and requested that Tibetan communities throughout the world collect funds for the relief effort.

After the events of 11 September 2001 in New York, the government of Tibet, although itself impoverished, immediately donated US$30,000 to the search and rescue effort. As the living embodiment of Chenrezig, the Dalai Lama demonstrates his kindness and compassion without exception or question.

The Dalai Lama has taken part in many interfaith conferences, and is keen to encourage understanding between the many faiths in the world. He has met the Pope at the Vatican on five occasions, as well as the Archbishop of Canterbury, and other important Anglican leaders. He has also met members of Jewish communities, and has spoken at a service held in his honour by the World Congress of Faiths.

He travels tirelessly, introducing the precious gems of the teachings of the Buddha, and seamlessly rendering them vital, true and fresh — pertinent to our modern life and mindsets. Huge crowds attend his teachings, many people travelling long distances to be blessed and inspired by him.

When he arrived in Melbourne in 1992 to give a public talk at the National Tennis Centre, a crowd of more than 22,000 people arrived to hear him talk, but the venue was not big enough to admit them all. Happily, the tour organising committee made urgent arrangements for his address to be broadcast to those standing outside.

Among his other responsibilities and teachings in 2001, the Dalai Lama taught in Tuscany, Italy, on Atisha's *Lamp for the Path to Enlightenment*, the same teaching he will give in Melbourne in 2002. In early 2001 he undertook a three-week, eight-city tour of the United States of America. Eighteen thousand people attended his public talk in California, 'Peace through Inner Peace'. Several thousand students took part in a youth forum with him, as he believes it is important to convey the messages of peace and inner satisfaction to younger people.

Every year the Dalai Lama gives teachings in India, and visits Bodhgaya, the place where the Shakyamuni Buddha reached enlightenment in 600 BCE.

The Dalai Lama has also taken part in scientific and mind science symposiums, and is the author of many books on Tibetan Buddhism. Many more books have been written about him, and collections of interviews, debates and transcripts of teachings have been published.

The Dalai Lama has visited Northern Ireland and other countries that have experienced war and conflict. He hopes that one day we may have a demilitarised world, a world without armaments and destruction.

He sees that issues such as poverty, hunger, overpopulation, environmental problems and disease are now global, transcending national boundaries. He believes that the only way to solve these issues is through our attainment of peaceful and happy minds. If our minds are at peace, and we have compassion, a peaceful and compassionate world will follow. The Dalai Lama, embodiment of Chenrezig, will then have achieved his dearest wish. His favourite prayer is from Shantideva's *The Bodhisattva's Way of Life*[2] and exemplifies all that is contained in the Mahayana Buddhist path.

> *For as long as space endures*
> *And for as long as sentient beings remain,*
> *Until then may I too abide,*
> *To dispel the misery of the world.*

A brief history of the Fourteenth Dalai Lama (1935–)

This Dalai Lama, like the historic Buddha, has known the extremes of human existence. He has lived through it all.

Tenzin Gyatso was born to be a ruler, to have everyone prostrate in his presence. Wherever he went, even as a small child, people treated him with utmost reverence. He was the highest ruler for the hundreds of thousands of Tibetan monks, nuns, scholars and ordinary Tibetans who were engaged in a collective process of awakening to the source of happiness. He was the ultimate guardian of a tradition two and a half thousand years old, in an unbroken lineage. His stewardship, which ensured the authenticity and depth of meditative experience, was a great responsibility. Yet he lost everything. When China invaded Tibet in 1950, the Dalai Lama lost his country and has not seen his homeland and his people — except for those in exile — for over forty years, since his exile in 1959. Thousands of monasteries were destroyed by the invading forces, millions of precious philosophical manuscripts and thousands of exquisite inspirational paintings and sculptures were lost forever. A whole civilisation of which he was the apex was forcibly and urgently dismantled.

All this was on the shoulders of the sixteen-year-old monk in the year Tibet's meditative silence was forever shattered when the Chinese army and the machine age roared in. A youth of sixteen had to decide what was best for six million people, for an entire civilisation and a land that had been sustainably managed by nomads who understood and respected its limits. He had to deal with the impatient invading nation, which saw his land as an unexploited commodity. China had little respect for Tibet's meditative traditions and the young Dalai Lama had to deal with the invading nation's doctrine that everything old had to be destroyed. Overnight he went from being the source of protection for all Tibetans to being China's largest concern and the focus of its might. Throughout it all, Buddhism was his guide and his source of inner strength.

At this time, the Dalai Lama still had years to go before fully completing the intensive studies that are part of the education of a great lama. He had never been beyond Tibet, which remained untouched by World War II. He longed to be a simple Buddhist monk, able to pursue a life of meditation and study. Seldom has such a burden fallen on one so young in the history of the world.

In 1951, the Chinese People's Liberation Army had destroyed the small Tibetan army and had taken command of the holy city of Lhasa. Two civilisations collided head on and the Dalai Lama was the point of impact. No longer did Tibet have the luxury of ignoring the world. To go on as before was not an option. The modern world, science, revolution, industri- alisation, speed and materialism had intruded, irreversibly. The Dalai Lama had to decide what could be done. In the film *Kundun*, drawn closely from the Dalai Lama's writings and recollections, we see how he grows and what he brings to this moment of decision, from which there is no turning back. When he is barely a teenager, his Lord Chamberlain reads to him the prophecy of the Great Thirteenth Dalai Lama, his immediate predecessor, warning of the disasters now beginning to happen. He listens, devastated.

'What can I do?' he says. 'I am only a boy.'

Without hesitation, his Lord Chamberlain says with confidence, 'You are the man who wrote this letter. You are the man who has come back to lead us. You will soon have great responsibilities. You must know what to do.'[3]

'Kundun' is one of many titles by which Tibetans know the Dalai Lama. It means 'Presence' in the Tibetan language. The Dalai Lama chooses to be present among us, as protector, although he has fully awoken and has complete freedom to exit the world of suffering. As a young monk, Tenzin Gyatso had to discover whether he could be that presence.

To be born Dalai Lama is to be Dalai Lama for life. It is not a position from which you can resign. To continue the work of a previous Dalai Lama and fulfil the needs of the people was an enormous burden.

At first, Tenzin Gyatso doubted he could live up to expectations as his people urged him to take on the full responsibilities of a Dalai Lama. This was not normally expected to occur until he turned eighteen. But there was no one else. He had to take the fate of a nation in his hands. He agreed to the great public ceremony in which he is handed the golden wheel, the symbol of his power over Tibet. After this his seal marked all official pronouncements. But time was short, and China's army was near so he had to prepare to flee towards India rather than be captured. But he soon returned to Lhasa, now occupied by the Chinese army, and for the next eight years there was an uneasy co-existence. China held back from implementing its revolutionary agenda, but the Dalai Lama's authority was being undermined.

The people of Tibet grew increasingly upset at the treatment they received from China's occupying force. The powerful Communist Party commanded the energies of the biggest nation on earth and was keen to implement communism in Tibet, to settle the nomads, bring in China's population overflow and remake Tibet in China's image. The Dalai Lama was the last source of Tibetan independence and for eight years he managed, by sheer presence of mind, to stave off the inevitable tragedy.

'China and Tibet are like fire and wood,' the Dalai Lama said, and it would not take much to reduce Tibet to ashes. There was no solution, no right answer. Small events suddenly assumed critical significance. The Dalai Lama had to make not one decision but thousands, any of which could be seen by China as intolerable. The monk Tenzin Gyatso and the powerful Chinese General Zhang were thrown together in Lhasa by history. There were no precedents to fall back on.

The Dalai Lama had only the weapons of the 'weak': delay, flexibility, negotiation, ambiguity, charm, wit and sensitivity. This was a time for the Buddhist practice of taking the enemy as the precious teacher of patience, in the face of provocation and unreasonable demands; much would have to be sacrificed if what really mattered was to have any chance of surviving.

The Dalai Lama has never regretted the many humilia-
tions. Not long after reaching exile, he wrote: 'I have no regret
at all that I followed the path of non-violence till the end.
From the all-important point of view of our religion, it was
the only possible policy.'[4]

What mattered most was the unbroken lineage of meditative awakening, transmitted from teacher to student since the
days of the Buddha. Nothing was more precious than maintaining the presence of fully enlightened teachers as guides and
protectors for all those who seek happiness.

All power belonged to China. The Dalai Lama could
not contradict Chinese announcements publicly and was soon
forced to sack his two prime ministers for showing too much
concern for Tibetan rights. The more the Tibetans placated the
Chinese, the more was demanded of them. In the end there
was nowhere to turn.

The film *Kundun* finishes with the Dalai Lama fleeing
from the Chinese, crossing the high Himalayan passes into
India, weak with illness. 'There was nothing dramatic about our
crossing of the frontier,' the Dalai Lama wrote not long after his
journey. 'The country was equally wild on each side of it, and
uninhabited. I saw it in a daze, of sickness and weariness, and
unhappiness deeper than I can express.'[5]

At the age of twenty-four, the Dalai Lama began life

again. He had escaped the Chinese armed forces with his life, but little else. Many urgent problems pressed on him. The survival of an entire culture was on his shoulders and he was still in his mid-twenties. Fellow refugees were in immediate danger. The plunge from high, dry, cold Tibet to hot, wet, monsoonal India, with refugees crammed into former prisoner-of-war camps, caused epidemics of infectious diseases to which Tibetans had little or no immunity. Many Tibetan refugees who had successfully evaded the Chinese army and survived the deep snows of the Himalayan passes, fell ill and died in India. The refugees were dependent on the kindness of India.

In Tibet the situation was unbearably worse. The Tibetans had struggled against China's military might and incurred the wrath of the Communist Party. The Dalai Lama could only look on helplessly from his place of exile:

'I do not think most people want to read of the extremes of cruelty, and I do not want to write of them ... Tens of thousands of our people have been killed, mainly and fundamentally because they would not renounce their religion ... Lamas have been specially persecuted ... especially the elderly and most respected ...'[6]

Everything the Dalai Lama had feared had happened. Everything the Thirteenth Dalai Lama had grimly prophesied was coming true. All the young Dalai Lama could do was to face the horror unflinchingly.

He persuaded India's Prime Minister Nehru that Tibetans needed to be in the mountains, not on the dusty plains and tropical jungles of India. Tibetan refugees were shifted to the mountains where they worked in road gangs, patiently cracking rocks into pieces small enough to make roadbed gravel, using only hammers as they squatted — whole families with young children — beside the newly forming roads into the Himalayas. It was better than the camps, but not much.

Refugees are the wretched of the earth, clinging to survival. The Dalai Lama told them to never give up, and it became his mantra. India offered land in the burning south, if the Tibetans were willing to clear dense jungle by hand and deal with wild elephants. Clearing meant burning. The Dalai Lama visited them, and recalled:

'There was not much I could do save give these pioneers every encouragement. I told them that we must not give up hope and assured them, hardly believing it myself, that in time we would be prosperous once more. I promised them that we would prevail. Fortunately, they believed every word I said and sure enough, little by little, their situation was transformed. Just as they had faith in me, I had faith in them.'[7]

He was quick to appreciate modernity. Rather than conceal things behind traditional rituals, he shared not only victory with others but also his doubts. He chose to be transparent about the difficulties of living up to expectations, no matter how hard it was to believe his own assurances. He began the process of removing protocol which had separated him from his people, saying:

'I had a strong feeling that we should not cling to old practices that were no longer appropriate. I was determined to be entirely open, to show everything and not hide behind etiquette. In this way I hoped that people would relate to me as one human being to another.'[8]

Transparency and openness and letting others see the inner workings behind the scenes are among the better aspects of our modern world and of democracy. The Dalai Lama quickly embraced them all, despite the shock this brought to his officials. In 1960, less than a year after fleeing Lhasa, he began the difficult process of full democratisation. 'The changes were so radical to Tibetans. Some of the older officials who had come into exile found these changes hard to accept at first.'[9]

In 1962, at the age of twenty-seven, the Dalai Lama wrote in his autobiography, *My Land and My People*, 'Certainly Tibet will never be the same again; but we do not want it to be. It can never again be isolated from the world, and it cannot return to its ancient semi-feudal system.'[10] He strode into the twentieth century as a messenger of peace and good-will to the world.

Opposite: The Dalai Lama
at Sarnath, India, 2000

Slowly, the Tibetans succeeded in re-establishing themselves, and today they are citizens of the world, readily at home any-where. Not only the great lamas but also many lay Tibetans have somehow been able to overcome the painful memories exiles bring into their new circumstances, and have devoted great energy to what essentially matters. As refugee survival was secured, they turned to rebuilding their monasteries so that the continuity of Buddhist practice and the lineages of practitioners could continue uninterrupted. In exile, the Tibetans have built and now fill and support more than three hundred monasteries.

Today Tibet, the Tibetan people and the Dalai Lama are well known, and Tibetan Buddhism is accessible and available world wide. The lamas who came into the modern world, experimenting — tentatively at first — with how to turn mod-ern minds, drew their inspiration from the Dalai Lama and his frequent theme of universal responsibility.

Their ability to put aside the self and their former status, and to drop all that is not truly of universal value are the clues to the quiet flowering of Tibetan Buddhism today. They saw that modern people were not troubled by where to find food, but instead were burdened by endless choice, by insula-tion from nature, by confusion about identity, and by material

Opposite: Four-armed Chenrezig,
the deity of compassion

abundance which never quite results in happiness. The lamas know that Buddhism is universally useful to all who suffer dissatisfaction, whether the origin seems to be external or internal, a lack of food or a restless mind. They bridged the cultural gaps and became living examples of a way to live without problems.

As early as 1963, the Dalai Lama wrote a book in which the entire Buddhist path is summarised concisely in all its diversity — *Opening the Eye of New Awareness*, which was written for people new to Buddhism. By the time the Dalai Lama first experienced the West, in 1973, he was ready to speak with the directness and simplicity which have made his message universal. He began by tackling directly the alienation of young people.

'I see nothing wrong with material progress provided man takes precedence over progress. In order to solve human problems in all their dimensions we must be able to combine and harmonise external material progress with inner mental development. Good human qualities — honesty, sincerity, a good heart — cannot be bought with money, nor can they be produced by machines, but only by the mind itself. Religion exists in order that you may practise something that will help you to control your mind; the aim is to transform the bad self-destructive thoughts into their direct opposites.'[11]

The Dalai Lama found himself in conversation with the human race, transcending difference and focusing on what we all have in common. He called his philosophy, and the book that came out of his first contact with Westerners, *Universal Responsibility and the Good Heart*.

The Great Thirteenth Dalai Lama (1877–1933)

Only two of the Dalai Lamas are known as Great — the Fifth and the Thirteenth. Almost certainly the present Dalai Lama will also be declared great, perhaps the greatest of all, but the present Dalai Lama and his immediate predecessor, Thubten Gyatso, share uncanny resemblances in their life stories.

The story of the Thirteenth Dalai Lama is of a Buddhist leader as remarkable as the Fourteenth; he was in many ways similar to the present Dalai Lama and in others quite unalike. Both were vigorous leaders and reformers. Both faced foreign invasion and were forced into exile. Both sought to modernise Tibet, yet maintain Buddhist practice intact. Both would have preferred a quiet contemplative monastic life, but were called on to protect their people. Both knew when to patiently accept what cannot be changed, and when to act boldly.

The biggest difference between the Thirteenth and Fourteenth Dalai Lamas is that the Thirteenth, with all the wealth, the people and Buddhist institutions of Tibet at his command, remained in a gilded cage of precedent and ritual, despite his energetic efforts to break through.

Looking back late in life, the Thirteenth Dalai Lama, Thubten Gyatso, recalled:

'When I reached the age of eighteen I was called upon to accept the responsibility of serving as spiritual and secular head of the country. I considered myself unqualified for the position, but because the political and religious leaders unanimously petitioned me to accept, and the Manchu emperor of China also urged me to do so, I felt there was no alternative but to agree.'[12]

The year was 1895 and British imperial power in India was at its height. The eighteen year old had by then, in his own words: 'applied myself ceaselessly day after day, year after year, to the vast corpus of spiritual teachings, until my mind was completely saturated with them.'[13] His training had been intensive, his discipline strong, his mind focused, supple, open and responsive. He was ready for what was to be a long reign of thirty-eight years.

Tibet at last had a Dalai Lama firmly in charge, after a long time. (After the Eighth Dalai Lama died in 1804 almost a century passed before another Dalai Lama sat firmly on the throne. The four Dalai Lamas after the Eighth and before the

Thirteenth all died young and had no opportunity to be effective.) The Thirteenth was robust, assertive, forthright, strong willed and determined to give Tibet leadership.

Tibet remained isolated and inward-looking, indifferent to the global tide of nationalism which was a preface to world war. Initially it seemed that Thubten Gyatso had plenty of time to complete the higher trainings of the mind that are valued so highly in Tibetan Buddhism. He planned to do a solitary retreat lasting over three years. All the signs were auspicious. By the age of twelve he had memorised and mastered long philosophical texts with such depth that he toured the great monasteries debating with the sharpest scholars.

Spiritually and psychologically he was ready to do the three-year retreat, and in 1903 he prepared to start. But, only months into his meditation retreat, the modern world erupted into Tibet, and his contemplative retreat came to a sudden end. The British empire was invading. So began a decade of invasions, in which the young Dalai Lama twice became a refugee.

Thubten Gyatso was born in the middle of Queen Victoria's long reign. India was the jewel in Britain's crown, and British officers keen for imperial adventure urged London to take Tibet into the British sphere of influence, if only to exclude the Russians. In 1903, as the British Indian army marched through the Himalayan passes into Tibet, the Thirteenth

Dalai Lama had ruled Tibet for eight peaceful years. For the first time in its history Tibet's great forts and monasteries, with rock walls metres thick, were defenceless in the face of modern artillery. Hundreds, perhaps thousands of Tibetans were massacred as the British pushed on, heading for the holy city of Lhasa.

The British arrived expecting to make the Tibetans sign a treaty submitting to British might but the Dalai Lama had disappeared as had all senior Tibetan officials. The British encountered a classic Buddhist method of dealing with aggression. No one responded to their aggression and the British had no choice but to wait. And wait. They waited months but there was no one to negotiate with, and they finally returned to India. This is the active non-violence which today's Dalai Lama champions, and which people sometimes mistake for weakness.

In the face of British military might the Tibetans were weak, yet their weakness was their strength as the British retreated empty handed. The crisis was over, and the Dalai Lama used the opportunity to travel widely in devoutly Buddhist Mongolia. Then he went on to counsel the aged Empress of China. As a refugee, he wrote a poem or song to sum up his life experience at the age of twenty-five:

> *When stability in training has been accomplished,*
> *One can easily transform as aids on the path*
> *All negative conditions and unpleasant events*

That arise to disturb the mind,
Such as illness, hindrances and problems.
Cultivate the ability to implement correctly
This essential oral instruction.

Although involvement in worldly concerns
Can bring some immediate superficial benefits,
In the long run it only harms us
And hinders our chances for enlightenment.

English translation fails to convey the poetic qualities of the verses, which make it easy for Tibetans to memorise and bring to mind when needed. For a twenty-five year old, it is bold advice for what needs to be done in order to be happy.[14]

The Thirteenth Dalai Lama was in exile a long time. The Chinese Emperor had invited the exiled Dalai Lama to Beijing, where he bestowed blessings on the old Empress and her nephew the Emperor. The Qing dynasty was in its dying days, but the British invasion stirred the Chinese empire. The British soldiers parading around Lhasa made China act, and caused the Thirteenth Dalai Lama his next crisis.

On his return to Lhasa, he found the city menaced by thousands of Chinese soldiers. The Chinese force was equipped with weapons far more modern and lethal than anything Tibet possessed. It had fought its way across Tibet for months, looting monasteries and executing Tibetans sent to negotiate peace. The Tibetan people were outraged.

As punishment for letting the British invade, China stripped the Dalai Lama of his title. The Tibetans ignored this. But the Chinese army marched into Lhasa, firing at the holiest of Buddhist temples and even the Dalai Lama's palace, the Potala.

Tibet was helpless, defenceless. The Dalai Lama, only two months back in Lhasa, had to flee again. Chinese troops pursued him, determined to capture or kill him. Everything was uncertain. Yet the Dalai Lama never felt a victim of circumstances. He insisted that whatever the situation, there was always a choice about how to respond.

If the Dalai Lamas were to endure and Tibetans remain the guardians of Tibet, he had to flee. It wasn't out of any personal fear for himself. He had a strong personality and was used to being in command. If he stayed, 'it would have been like the rubbing out of a footprint,' he said, referring to the first symbol of the Buddha.

The Dalai Lama went south, towards the Himalayas and India. As the Himalayas rose before him, he had to decide whether to take the easier route to refuge in the independent Buddhist kingdom of Bhutan or go on through the Himalayas in midwinter, in the hope of reaching India. Numb with cold, he found a way to make his decision. He closed his eyes. If he

could bring the tips of his forefingers to meet before his fore-
head, he would press on into the deep snow-drifts of the high
pass to India.

'The tips met; so he decided to face the forty miles
instead of only two. When he came safely through, the Tibetans
took it as another sign he was a real incarnation of Chenrezig.'[15]
So wrote his friend Charles Bell.

It was a gamble. Would the British take advantage of his
weakness? Would China entrench itself in Lhasa? Everything
hinged on the Dalai Lama and one Englishman entrusted with
liaison, interpreting and negotiating. That person was Charles
Bell. They got on well, and the friendship of the two men did
much to soften Britain's official ideology. Britain considered
that the world was divided up between the great nations, such
as Britain, Russia and China, and that Tibet could belong to
only one of these. All the British cared about was to make sure
Russia had no say in Tibet; if China asserted control, that was
fine. Despite this, Charles Bell did all he could for the Dalai
Lama.

The Dalai Lama had to be patient towards his enemies,
and not see himself as their victim. Years later, not long before
his death, he wrote:

'Under those circumstances there was really nothing we
could do, other than sit and pray for a favourable change in the

nature of the situation. And our prayers were soon answered, for the profound power of truth is great, and the forces of karma infallible.'[16]

The Dalai Lama spent four or five hours daily in meditation and creative visualisation practice. He recalled Atisha's teachings on how to change adverse circumstances into the path to enlightenment. These practices of thought transformation utilise any and all immediate circumstances as objects of meditation to dissolve the seeming solidity of whatever wrongs have been done.

Britain had gone to war against Tibet under the command of Lord Curzon, but Curzon was now in disgrace, and Lord Minto, his replacement, was not given to grand fantasies. He wanted Britain to be a friendly nation. The Dalai Lama met Britain's Viceroy who was in command of India. A seventeen-gun salute accompanied his introduction to Lord Minto, with Charles Bell present as interpreter.

The Dalai Lama decided the best policy was to accept British hospitality and wait, giving the Chinese space. He waited two years. During that time the last Chinese dynasty fell, and Chinese soldiers mutinied and turned on each other, or deserted, returning to their families in China. Despite their lack of modern weapons, Tibetan soldiers regained confidence and repeatedly ambushed Chinese troops. Finally, with the Chinese on the verge of collapse, the Dalai Lama returned home. China's new rulers restored his titles, but to the Tibetans he had remained Dalai Lama throughout, protector of his people.

China's ambition of colonising Tibet had, in the Dalai Lama's words, 'faded like a rainbow in the sky'. The Tibetans could rebuild, and the Great Thirteenth Dalai Lama ruled for a further twenty years. He revived Tibetan sacred dance rituals, supervised the academic standards of training the teachers of high philosophy, cracked down on corruption, painted, learned all he could of the world, composed songs and poetry, wrote philosophical texts and commentaries on the classics, and was the patron of an artistic revival. He reformed Tibet, supervising the monasteries, maintaining a daily meditation practice, teaching Buddhist texts and attending to his many other responsibilities.

After the British and Chinese invasions, Tibet could never be the same. Thubten Gyatso knew that Tibet, once famed for its seclusion, would have to find its way in the modern world. In his last testament, he urged Tibet to face its dangers.

'In the present age the five great degenerations seem to totally dominate life on earth, to the extent that fighting and conflict have become part of the very fabric of human society. If we do not make preparations to defend ourselves from the overflow of violence, we will have very little chance of survival.'[17]

Tibetans could not imagine the violence of the world overflowing into Tibet and never built a modern army. Tibet needed translators, radio engineers, mineral geologists and other skills. In 1933, not long after the Thirteenth Dalai Lama issued his warning he died. When China did invade, the next Dalai Lama was almost old enough to take charge.

Tibetans look back on the accomplishments of the Great Thirteenth Dalai Lama with deep respect. Taktser Rinpoche, elder brother of the present Dalai Lama says, 'The fact that all these things were done by one man is amazing. Each of these spheres of activity would require a complete lifetime for an ordinary person. His accomplishments were like those of ten great men.'[18]

Those who came in contact with him were in no doubt they had experienced enlightenment not as a theory, or a philosophy, but as an embodied lived reality. This Dalai Lama had the confidence, strength and clarity to be what the times demanded, to be almost all things to all people. An enlightened person can be a capable, decisive leader fulfilling many roles, as circumstances require, because there is no essential self behind the roles, leaving room for them to be what the situation demands.

The Thirteenth and Fourteenth Dalai Lamas both loved gardening and tinkering with modern technologies. Both had the knack of appearing to others in a familiar, relaxed way, according to what people responded to most readily. Both knew when to act decisively, and when to bide their time patiently. Both Dalai Lamas became refugees. They were modern, adaptable and unsentimental about the past and made lasting friendships across cultures and personal difference. Both relied on the weapons of the 'weak', on non-violence, and wrote many philosophical texts and inspiring poetry to show how to live authentically, in freedom and happiness under even the most extreme circumstances. They embody and have lived enlightened lives, inspiring others to do the same.

Perhaps the deepest connection between the two lies in the final prophetic testament of the Thirteenth Dalai Lama, which specified in uncanny detail the events that would be at the centre of his successor's life. In 1931, Thubten Gyatso wrote:

'In particular, we must guard against the barbaric red communists, who carry terror and destruction with them wherever they go. They are the worst of the worst. Already they have consumed much of Mongolia. It will not be long before we find the red onslaught at our own front door. Even the names of the Dalai and Panchen Lamas will be erased, as will those of the other lamas, lineage-holders and holy beings. The monasteries will be looted and destroyed, and the monks and nuns killed or chased away. The great works of the noble Dharma kings of old will be undone, and all of our cultural and spiritual institutions persecuted, destroyed and forgotten. The birth-right and property of the people will be stolen; we will become like slaves to our conquerors, and made to wander helplessly like beggars. Everyone will be forced to live in misery, and the days and nights will pass slowly and with great suffering and terror.'[19]

Two years later, the Thirteenth Dalai Lama died, and two years later the next Dalai Lama was born, and when he reached the age of sixteen the prophecy became reality.

Atisha (982–1054)

A thousand years ago, an Indian Buddhist monk named Atisha travelled from India to the southern hemisphere and then on to the high alpine meadows of Tibet. Travel to such remote regions from the Indian heartland of Buddhism was dangerous and difficult. These two journeys were undertaken in the second half of his life.

On his first voyage, Atisha sailed across the equator to the Buddhist kingdom of Great Victory (*Srivijaya*) — today's Sumatra, Indonesia — to find a teacher who could help him liberate his mind. At the time Buddhism in India was in decline and the number of Indian teachers whose lives exemplified the teachings was dwindling. Atisha was already a renowned teacher in India, but he was determined to attain enlightenment in one lifetime, and this took him across seas that were reputed to be full of dangerous pirates and monsters. Atisha took these risks because there was a teacher in the Golden Island so inspiring and incisive that he could lead meditators to full enlightenment. His second journey was across the Himalayas into Tibet. He went at the invitation of the King of Western Tibet who requested Atisha to re-establish the Buddha's teachings in Tibet.

In the Buddhist kingdom of Srivijaya, Atisha found Dharmakirti, a teacher whose penetrating insight enabled students to free themselves from all unhappiness, hope and fear. Srivijaya practised not an imitative provincial Buddhism but a wholehearted commitment, at all levels of society, to awaken to happiness. The son had surpassed the Indian father.

At this time, Buddhism in India was one and a half thousand years old, but was dying out as Afghan raiders penetrated further into India, destroying monasteries. On the Golden Island of Sumatra, Buddhism was practised with vigour and purpose. Srivijaya was extraordinarily wealthy, and the kings of Srivijaya regularly paid homage to the sea by sharing their wealth with it. Rather than accumulating wealth as an end in itself, the richest citizens of Srivijaya threw bricks of gold into the waters daily, honouring the source of all their riches.

Srivijaya's wealth came from trade. The presence of Buddhism in this golden time was no accident, because Srivijaya's success was based on converting the plunder of the seas into regular trade, which meant converting the pirates to peaceable ways. Buddhist meditators with powers similar to Atisha tamed the minds of the nomadic pirates who had plagued these waters. The Srivijaya kingdom, which lasted 350 years, never forced these nomads to settle or abandon their life on the sea. Instead their energies were turned to good use, fostering trade and prosperity based on their intimate knowledge of the seas and the innumerable islands.

Atisha's biographers wrote as much about his thirteen-month voyage to the southern hemisphere as they did about the twelve years he was there with his teacher. The voyage was a great quest, a time of testing, purification and ultimately a triumph of the power of loving kindness over violence. Significantly, the present Dalai Lama, who is seen as an incarnation of the deity of compassion, often speaks of love as a real force in the world, capable of overcoming hatred at all levels. Atisha is a cultural hero to Tibetans because he never wavered in his certainty that compassion is relevant, useful and powerful in all situations.

In the Tibetan biography of Atisha, the climax of his

life story is his arrival before his new teacher, celebrated in lengthy verses as they greet each other with operatic eloquence. Atisha was already an accomplished meditator, able to tame demons with the power of his unconditional loving kindness and compassion. The teachings he received in Srivijaya were on how we make our world, how things exist, and how our unhappiness and the complexity of the world originate in our desire to exist as separate selves. Atisha sought profound insight into the nature of being, a penetrating wisdom at the core of Buddhism. The Dalai Lama calls this 'special insight'. He learned that all that arises, all that appears, is emptiness. As the *Heart Sutra* says:

> *There are no characteristics.*
> *There is no birth and no cessation.*
> *There is no impurity and no purity.*
> *There is no decrease and no increase.*
> *In emptiness, there is no ignorance, no end of ignorance,*
> *no old age and death, no end of old age and death;*
> *no suffering, no origin of suffering, no cessation of suffering,*
> *no path, no wisdom, no attainment, and no non-attainment.*

Atisha developed wisdom to match his compassion. He was ready to return to central Asia, where he composed the *Lamp for the Path to Enlightenment*.

Tibet took to Buddhism later than its neighbouring countries. By Atisha's time, China had been Buddhist for eight centuries, India for 1500 years and Tibet's inner-Asian neighbours had long been Buddhist also. In Tibet there had been a popular embrace of Buddhism but also strong resistance, in part based on a realistic fear that a Buddhist Tibet would no longer maintain the military might of Tibetan conquests. But one of the local kings was willing to spend his entire fortune, if need be, to bring Atisha to Tibet. He sent a skilful negotiator, Nagtso, to India to try to persuade Atisha and his Indian meditation masters, whose permission was needed, that Atisha should make the journey to Tibet.

We know what sort of person Atisha was because we have Nagtso's own impressions of Atisha from a thousand years ago. Without knowing how to recognise Atisha, Nagtso watched as Buddhist monks, scholars and great meditators assembled in the hall of the famous Indian monastery of Vikramashila. Nagtso later wrote in a letter addressed to Atisha:

'As all the rows of participants had joined the assembly, you, Lord, appeared, and I could not gaze at you enough. To Indians looking at you, you looked Indian, to Nepalis and Tibetans and to the gods, as they beheld you, you looked Nepali and Tibetan and a god alike. Besides the great splendour of your appearance, there was a smile on your face: your robes were smooth as if polished. You walked without haughtiness, your walk was gentle, the king in person rose from his seat.'[20]

In Tibet, Atisha found another nomadic people, on grasslands as vast as the Indian Ocean. Like the seafarers of Sumatra, the Tibetans were wild, and in need of the teachings that turn the mind towards balance and the happiness that comes from within. Atisha achieved much in Tibet. He taught how to work with the rich diversity of Buddhist approaches. In the twelve years he spent in Tibet, he ensured that the entire range of Buddhist teachings, methods, practices, paths and meditative lineages struck fertile ground. A huge variety of methods became available, according to individual ability, which Atisha presented in a way similar to the life cycle; starting with basic practices suited to beginners and graduating to more directly effective methods which required greater concentration, clarity and stability of mind. His systematic approach culminated in the most direct methods of awakening and of transforming habits, which also required the greatest dedication and motivation. This entire cycle is compressed into his *Lamp for the Path to Enlightenment*.

Like Atisha, the Dalai Lama is known for his gentleness, informality and lack of haughtiness. He sums up Atisha's teachings:

'Some people, especially those who see themselves as very realistic and practical, may think: "This idea of wishing for the happiness of all sentient beings and this idea of cultivating thoughts of cherishing the well-being of all sentient beings are unrealistic and too idealistic. They don't contribute in any way to the transformation of one's mind or to attaining some kind of mental discipline because they are completely unachievable." In a way that may be a valid objection, but what is important here is to understand the impact of cultivating such altruistic sentiments.

'The point is to try to develop the scope of one's empathy in such a way that it can extend to any form of life that has the capacity to feel pain and experience happiness. This kind of sentiment is very powerful, and effective.'[21]

Atisha and the Dalai Lama are two Buddhist practitioners whose lives have shown how powerful and effective compassion and wisdom are. Their presence brings enlightenment into our lives as a tangible energy, inspiring us to aim for the same awakening.

The Way Forward

The lives of the Thirteenth and Fourteenth Dalai Lamas encompass the whole twentieth century, which has been a turbulent century in Tibetan, Buddhist and world history. What the Thirteenth Dalai Lama prophesied in 1931 remains largely true over seventy years later. The Dalai Lama remains deeply concerned about the survival of Tibetan civilisation, and its contribution to the world. He invites the world to share his concern, and promotes dialogue wherever possible. He urges us to consider the survival of an authentically Tibetan Tibet.

'Tibetan political status is of course important, but to keep alive the Tibetan spirit, the Tibetan cultural heritage, that's my main concern. This not only benefits the six million Tibetan people, but also is of interest to the larger community — particularly, in the long run, to the Chinese. There are millions of young Chinese who are sometimes called the "Lost Generation". In that vacuum, Tibetan Buddhist culture can make a contribution.'[22]

Buddhism is central to the Dalai Lama's belief in active non-violence as an effective solution. With extraordinary patience, he seeks a long-term resolution acceptable to all, rather than a shorter-term victory in which there are winners and losers. Some Tibetans are understandably frustrated that four decades of non-violence have produced no result, but the Dalai Lama never gives up.

The Dalai Lama and his prime minister, Samdhong Rinpoche, take inspiration from Gandhi, who not only pressured the British to quit India but delayed that victory by decades rather than have popular emotions flare into uncontrolled violence. Gandhi called his approach an experiment with truth, and the Dalai Lama has a similar belief that truth will succeed in the end.

That belief arises from the Buddhist belief that all our delusions are just clouds, temporarily obscuring the sun. The human mind is like the sun, infinitely creative, resourceful, imaginative, expressive, capable and connected: our ideologies, individual beliefs and habits of mind are the clouds which disperse of their own accord if given space. To awaken to the full capacity of the mind is as natural as the sun coming out from behind a cloud. This is why the Dalai Lama remains optimistic. Recently, he said, 'Truth has its own strength. So as time goes by, something truthful starts to grow, becomes stronger and stronger.'[23]

In his global conversation with humanity the Dalai Lama touches our hearts, so that we can open to ourselves and our wider circumstances. The Dalai Lama has a far broader agenda than freedom for his people. If there is a non-violent resolution to the conflict in Tibet, it will send a message to people everywhere that non-violence is a real alternative to meeting aggression with aggression. So keen is the Dalai Lama on a non-violent solution as an example for warring parties around the world that, like Gandhi, he might prefer a longer wait if the result is lasting.

'Our ultimate goal should be the demilitarisation of the entire planet. If it were properly planned and people were educated to understand the advantages I believe it would be quite possible. But if we are to have the confidence to eliminate physical weapons, to begin with some kind of inner disarmament is necessary. We need to embark on the difficult task of developing love and compassion within ourselves. Compassion is, by nature, peaceful and gentle, but it is also very powerful.'[24]

People often think the Dalai Lama's global role, teaching

basic goodness and universal responsibility, is quite separate from his role as campaigner for human rights and leader of the Tibetans. But they are inseparable. Sometimes he quotes his hero, Mahatma Gandhi, who said: 'Those who think religion is separate from politics, don't know the first thing ... about religion.'[25]

Right now the modern interest in Buddhism and the plight of Tibet may seem far apart, one personal, the other political. But, the Dalai Lama reminds us, the power of non-violence is the power of truth, mobilised and expressed so all can hear. We don't see exactly what the Dalai Lama may yet accomplish but the momentum is growing, and he says he has many years in him yet.

We all feel the need for a world leader who is wise, kindly, practical and benevolent, reminding us of what really matters. This is what the Dalai Lama has become and he has a unique role in our globalising, interdependent world.

The Dalai Lama suggests simply that you be yourself, accept and fully experience yourself and your world, come home to who you are, and calmly make whatever changes are needed to live more wholesomely and helpfully. We can pray that he enjoys a long life, for the sake of all sentient beings, without exception.

CHAPTER THREE

HAPPINESS IN A MATERIAL WORLD: A teaching by the Fourteenth Dalai Lama

*We all want happiness, and do not want suffering, but we
encounter ceaseless streams of suffering. If we try to find out
where these sufferings come from, we realise that the source is
within us. The internal afflictive emotions residing within our
own minds are the real source of trouble … The cause is not
our so-called external enemy … The whole of Buddhist
teaching is actually the method or mechanism to combat our
internal enemy.* — The Dalai Lama

In 1996 the Dalai Lama visited Australia and New Zealand,
teaching, giving public talks and meeting many people. Wherever
he went, he spoke strongly in favour of world peace, love, compassion and the importance of tolerance and understanding for
people of different faiths and backgrounds. His visit culminated
in the bestowing of the Kalachakra initiation in Sydney, and

the teachings in this chapter are taken from the preliminary teachings he gave in the days preceding the initiation. More than four thousand people attended the Kalachakra teachings which lasted eight days; days filled with colour, ritual and blessings, and the profound teachings of the Buddha. Included in the following section are a few of the questions asked of the Dalai Lama, and excerpts from the preliminary teachings given over three days.

The Dalai Lama's teachings

Before I teach, I would like to explain why I prostrate to the throne before I sit on it. This tradition is rather useful. Firstly, we show reverence to the seat on which the teacher will sit and give the teaching in order to show respect for the teaching and for Buddha himself. Even the Buddha Shakyamuni himself, before he gave a ceremony or teachings, prepared the seat in order to show respect to the teachings. The essential thing is that according to Buddhism the real refuge, where all the protection is, is not Buddha but Dharma. So even Buddha him-self showed respect towards Dharma. Since we follow the Buddha, before giving teachings we must pay respect to the teachings and to the Buddha. That's one purpose of prostration.

The second purpose is that there's the danger that once you sit in a higher position you may feel, 'Oh, now for today at least, for a short period, I'm sort of superior.' That kind of negative emotion may develop. In order to counter that, firstly, one must show respect to the teachings as well as to Buddha and also to the figures in the lineage. And then one may sit on the throne and recite some verses and then meditate on impermanence.

Different faiths

There's no doubt that tantric teachings such as the Kalachakra are very famous and have a strong attraction for people. But I personally believe that the introductory and preliminary Buddhist teachings are more effective and beneficial in our day-to-day life. Tantric teachings are a very complex kind of practice, and quite difficult to do. The preliminary teachings actually deal with our day-to-day experience. In order to be a genuine follower of Buddha, they show what should be done and what we should keep in our minds, every day and every night.

There is one thing I would like to make clear at the beginning. I believe that among humanity there are so many different mental dispositions, and therefore in the past, at different places and at different times, many different spiritual traditions have developed. Generally speaking, if there's a healthier or better or safer way to follow your religion or to have religious faith, it is better to follow that way. Certain people change their religious faith and sometimes eventually find more confusion in their minds. So, to those people who are traditionally not Buddhist, sometimes I do feel a little hesitation in explaining about the Buddhadharma (Buddhist teachings).

Of course, for the Chinese and Vietnamese and perhaps some other people who are traditionally closer to Buddhism, there is no problem. I would like to clarify that all the world's major religious traditions have more or less the same potential to help and serve humanity and to transform people into better warm-hearted persons. The variety of religions is necessary because of the variety of mental dispositions. I think the concept of one truth or one religion for all humanity as a whole is difficult to accept. It's like taking medicine. Sometimes a particular medicine is the only medicine which can cure a particular illness. We cannot say that this medicine is the only medicine that exists. But under particular circumstances, for one particular patient this medicine is the only medicine that can cure this illness. Similarly, for an individual, according to his or her mental disposition, this religion is the only truth.

The concept of only one religion existed in ancient times where people lived in isolation with no connection with people from other religious traditions. Then it was perfectly suitable to have only one religion; in fact I think that concept increased their faith. So then it was very good.

We must be respectful towards all the world's major religious traditions.

Today things are much changed, and the concept of one truth or one religion is now rather difficult to apply. We must be respectful towards all the world's major religious traditions. Out of millions of people from those areas traditionally not Buddhist, some people may of course feel that the Buddhist approach is more suitable or effective. In that case, it is the individual's right to adopt Buddhism as their personal religion. But it is not advisable to adopt Buddhism hurriedly; you find some new book, think it looks good and then immediately take it as your personal religion. That kind of attitude is not good.

The matter of changing your religion is a big decision. Therefore it is very, very important to think very carefully and think, think and wait. Once you are really convinced that the new religious tradition, such as Buddhism, is more suitable and effective, then of course you can adopt that as a new religion. But after this it is very important to keep in mind that, because of human nature, there's a possibility or danger that you may become critical about your previous religion or tradition in order to justify your new decision. We must avoid such things, because at this time we are trying to promote religious understanding among the different traditions. In such a period, having critical views of one another is very harmful. Secondly, in order to show respect for others' views or rights, and to practise the spirit of pluralism, we must respect other religious traditions.

Happiness

We are definitely not born into this world to bring destruction or harm to other people, but to lead a more meaningful life. From the Buddhist viewpoint, in this life, from the start of existence on this planet, we are something like tourists. I think our maximum stay is about a hundred years! It's just a short visit on this planet. So I think we should be wise tourists. When we visit some other places in the world, we behave well and enjoy ourselves to the maximum. Similarly, whether we like it or not, I think that's the way we exist on this planet — not for destruction, not for causing harm to others. So be a nice warm-hearted, sensible person; that's very important.

We all want happiness and do not want suffering, but we

Above: The Dalai Lama
and the Kalachakra sand
mandala, Sydney, 1996.
Left and *below:* The
Kalachakra teachings,
Sydney, 1996.

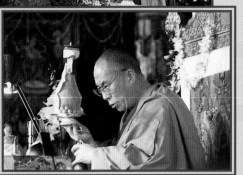

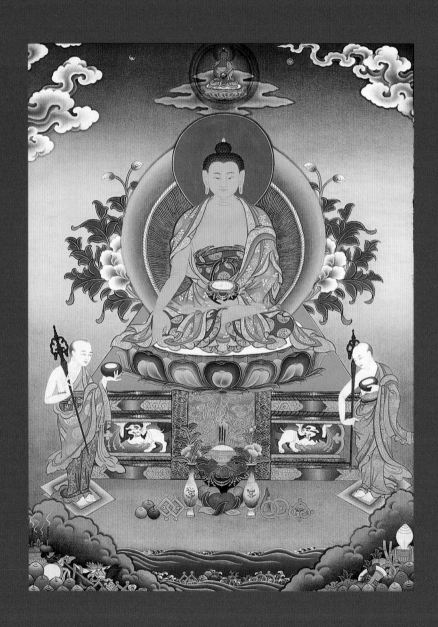

encounter ceaseless streams of suffering. If we try to find out where these sufferings come from, we realise that the source is within us. The internal afflictive emotions residing within our own minds are the real source of trouble or suffering. This is very dangerous for us; it destroys our happiness. The cause is not our so-called external enemy. If that were the case, we could escape it or cheat it or take some countermeasure. We could physically deal with it. In ancient times they constructed castles! And I think in modern times these are constructed with better foundations.

In some way, we can deal with the external enemy, but the enemy that is inside our own mind is difficult. Wherever we live, wherever we go, it is always there. And it is also very difficult to identify these afflictive emotions like anger, hatred and attachment. When they appear, they seem to be a very close friend or protector; that is the way they cheat us. The aim or goal of practising the teachings of the Buddha is liberation from these afflictive emotions. The whole of Buddhist teaching is actually the method or mechanism to combat our internal enemy.

In Buddhism, the actual Dharma is liberation, a state where we are free from afflictive emotions. Likewise the Dharma is the true path which leads to the achievement of such a state of liberation. The other kind of Buddhist spiritual practices,

Opposite: Shakyamuni Buddha

which lead only to the attainment of higher status, or higher rebirth like the birth of a human being or a god, are not the ultimate or actual Dharma.

Motivation

Whatever activities we do, and whether they become positive or negative, very much depend on our motivation. So in order to make our practices become positive Dharma, it's extremely important first of all to cultivate positive mental attitudes. It is because of this in Tibet that we have the tradition of reciting the verse which involves taking refuge to Buddha, Dharma and Sangha, and the cultivation of altruism to achieve enlightenment for the sake of all sentient beings. While we recite this verse it's extremely important for both the teacher and the student to cultivate the right and proper motivation.

Achieving long-term happiness

All sentient beings, including human beings, innately long for happiness and do not want suffering. This natural aspiration to have happiness and to shun suffering is absolutely right. In fact, it is also right to make an attempt to have the maximum amount of happiness and to put an end to our suffering. Regarding the processes of achieving happiness and of removing suffering, there are different levels. One level is when people try to achieve temporary happiness and on the way put an end to suffering. However, this is very shortsighted, and because of this fact there's every likelihood that this might invite more suffering and more trouble.

We have problems in the family, in society and in nations. If we look carefully we'll find that all these problems are the result of the shortsighted pursuit of happiness. We engage in certain kinds of processes of accumulating more wealth, or of gaining victories over others. We do not do this necessarily to inflict something upon ourselves but in order to have a kind of happiness. But because of this shortsighted attempt and following a wrong procedure, instead of gaining happiness we accumulate more and more suffering. Therefore, it is extremely important to follow a path or to pursue a life in which we will achieve both temporary and long-term happiness; happiness for ourselves and happiness for other sentient beings. Even in the case where you have to sacrifice certain temporary happiness, if this leads to achievement of long-lasting happiness it is worthwhile following such a path.

... if there's no peace and happiness within our mind this dominant experience of mental suffering or unhappiness will not enable us to enjoy physical comfort.

We experience two levels of happiness and suffering — mental and physical. Of these, it's important to pay greater attention to the experience of suffering and happiness of the mind than the physical experience of happiness and suffering. The indication that the mental experiences are more important than the physical ones is that even if we're encountering a certain physical discomfort or suffering, provided our mind is at ease, relaxed, calm and stable, we will be able to deal effectively with the physical suffering. On the other hand, even if we have a lot of physical comfort and may be enjoying our beautiful environment and surroundings, if there's no peace and happiness within our mind this dominant experience of mental suffering or unhappiness will not enable us to enjoy physical comfort. This clearly indicates the importance of mental experience over physical experience.

If there's a clash between our temporary experience and our permanent experience of happiness and suffering, it's extremely important to pay attention to the permanent experience. If we have to sacrifice a certain temporary happiness in order to achieve long-term happiness, it's worthwhile to do so. And even if we're enjoying wonderful temporary happiness, if that leads to suffering then it's worthwhile removing that temporary happiness in the pursuit of long-term happiness.

However, in case you see something which provides

temporary and long-term happiness, then that's the best! On the other hand, if something looks quite good in the long run but is temporarily difficult, we have to put up with the temporary difficulties or pain in order to safeguard the long-term benefit.

Taking refuge in the Three Jewels

All the major religious traditions of the world speak about an object of refuge; by confiding or trusting in that object of refuge, the followers take a systematic path. It's a natural tendency of sentient beings, including the tiniest insect, to seek refuge when they encounter something frightening.

Based on this natural tendency to want happiness and avoid suffering, human beings try their best to obtain the maximum amount of happiness and to remove suffering. But there's a limitation to the human capacity. When they reach that limitation, they turn to a transcendental state of power for refuge.

Here we're speaking about the process of taking refuge in accordance with the Buddha's teaching. Historically, we have Shakyamuni Buddha who in the initial stage was Prince Siddhartha, and who became enlightened through spiritual practice and purification. Through his enlightened mind and energy and because of the way he expressed things to others, people started to take refuge in Buddha. In accordance with the Buddha's own experience and the path along which he travelled, he taught his followers the process of disciplining and purifying the mind, body and speech. Based on that, the followers of the Buddha came into existence, who are the object of refuge called the Sangha.

Both the Buddha and Sangha became objects of refuge and trust because of a certain inner quality of discipline. That inner quality was called Dharma. So Dharma is a stage of having removed the afflictive emotions, a cessation of the negative state of the mind. And Dharma is the actual object of refuge. It is called 'the actual object of refuge' because whoever possesses such a state of mind of having removed the afflictive emotions is then totally free from suffering, and fear.

Neither the Buddha nor Sangha were the object of trust or refuge in the initial stage. Buddha was not an enlightened being right at the beginning. Both the Buddha and Sangha were just ordinary beings like us, with delusions and afflictive emotions. Through following the path and purifying their minds, they became enlightened.

Achieving enlightenment means achieving a state of total purification of the negative emotions within the mind.

What Buddha actually taught us was his life's experience. Buddha became enlightened at Bodhgaya in India. What do we mean by achieving enlightenment? Achieving enlightenment means achieving a state of total purification of the negative emotions within the mind. This process is achieved through the cultivation of positive practices and qualities — that is, the cultivation of calm abiding and special insight. That means single-pointed meditation, seeing reality as it really is through insight or wisdom. How did Buddha get into such a practice?

Buddha started cultivating calm abiding and special insight because of his experience of seeing the four great sights: the suffering of old age, sickness and death, and also seeing a monk who seemed completely at peace and happy. Buddha was wise enough to find out the causes of these sufferings of old age, sickness and death. He found that the causes of all these problems lie in the very path that we take in cyclic existence.

The question is how that path came into existence. The path is the result of negative causes and conditions. The cause, in fact, is the deluded state of the mind, which fundamentally rests in ignorance. He found that the only way to put an end to ignorance is through the cultivation of wisdom. Seeing reality and cultivating wisdom is possible if we're able to cultivate a strong one-pointed meditation. This is the way that Buddha became enlightened.

A great Indian scholar mentioned in one of his texts that Buddha, Dharma and Sangha are objects of refuge for those desiring total liberation from cyclic existence. Therefore, it's extremely important for us, first of all, to investigate how Buddha, Dharma and Sangha became the infallible objects of refuge. For this we need to have a good understanding of the Four Noble Truths.

Also, when we talk about Buddha, Dharma and Sangha as the ultimate object of refuge, as I explained earlier, the actual object of refuge is Dharma. The reason is that we find out whether someone is an enlightened being or not based on the investigation of the teaching being taught by that being. If that teaching proves to be correct, unmistaken and infallible, then the teacher or the Buddha can be accepted as an enlightened being. But if the teaching is found to be incorrect or mistaken, we cannot accept such a teacher as infallible, correct, valid or reliable.

Buddha himself taught that all wise people should judge his teaching just like a goldsmith judges gold, by putting it under fire, rubbing it and cutting it. Likewise, he told his followers to judge his teaching and not follow it just out of respect. Because of this, among the followers of the Buddha there were eminent scholars like Arya Nagarjuna, Aryadeva and so forth, who by following the teaching of the Buddha thoroughly investigated and experimented through their own experience. Based on their own personal experiments and investigation, they composed wonderful texts and teachings. These are a kind of eye-opener for us to follow the path of reasoning and logic.

Many of Buddha's followers achieved what we call arhathood. Arhathood means a state where they have thoroughly destroyed the afflictive emotions, which Buddha himself had achieved. It's important for us to investigate whether there's any difference between the arhathood achieved by his followers and that achieved by the Buddha himself. If we find a difference or superiority, we should investigate how this difference came into being, and the different techniques or processes they followed. According to the historical account, Buddha was an ordinary being like us. Through following a path of practice and spiritual purification, he finally became enlightened in Bodhgaya.

Now let us experiment with our own very limited, minor experiences. For example, if we reflect and meditate sincerely on compassion, loving kindness and the profound view of reality or emptiness, we will be able to get some positive energy or positive feeling. When we make a constant effort to transform our mental attitude mainly through the practice of altruism, we should investigate the reason why we need altruism. What is the benefit that we get from the actual practice of altruism? How can it transform us? Now here, according to the teaching of Nagarjuna, when we investigate and meditate on this, there's definitely some effect. Altruism can change our whole attitude towards ourselves and others. Based on that genuine meditation and practice, we do get some positive feelings; a sense of well-being, security and achievement. If, even in our ordinary case and through such a limited short practice, we're able to get some feeling of positive energy or achievement, based on this we can infer the possibilities of higher achievement by those teachers who have been undergoing spiritual practice for a long time.

What's important is that we should engage personally in sincere, genuine practice. Based on that practice, we will be able to gain some insight or taste the flavour of our practice and get some experience. That experience will give us confidence in the validity or perfect teaching of the lama. Then we are able to see the treatises or commentaries of the followers of the Buddha as valid, and thereby we find the Mahayana teachings taught by the Buddha to be valid teachings.

To come back to the point from where we started, the Buddha, Dharma and Sangha are the objects of refuge for those desiring liberation. This means that by depending on the Buddha, Dharma and Sangha, we'll be able to achieve this state of liberation or total cessation of afflictive emotions. The process of taking refuge in Dharma actually means that we should personally cultivate that state of Dharma within ourselves, because this will protect us.

Taking refuge in Dharma involves two processes. One is the true path which we have to cultivate, and which leads to the cessation of afflictive emotions. Then by following such a path, we achieve freedom from fear and suffering. That state of true cessation is also called Dharma because it actually is a state where we have no fear or fright. Through the process of actually cultivating these positive paths and the states of true cessation of afflictive emotions, we become protected. There's no other way of protecting ourselves.

> We ourselves are our own masters and
> everything rests on our own shoulders.
> If we do not behave well, nobody can
> save us or protect us. Ultimately it
> depends on our heart.

The conclusion is that basically Buddhists believe in some kind of self-creation. Therefore, the ultimate protector is oneself. We ourselves are our own masters and everything rests on our own shoulders. If we do not behave well, nobody can save us or protect us. Ultimately it depends on our heart.

In Buddhism in general, and particularly in the Mahayana Buddhist tradition, it is extremely important to analyse, investigate and experiment with the teachings. Through experimentation and investigation, if you find that the teaching is logical and reasonable then you should accept it. And if you do not find it logical and reasonable, in that case you should categorise it as a teaching of the interpretative level.

At the same time it is also extremely important to realise that there's a level of phenomena called 'completely hidden phenomena'. Those phenomena could be completely hidden because of their very subtle nature, and they also could be hidden phenomena because of our own limited level of progress of the mind. At such a point, we may not be able to establish this with reason and logic. But being unable to prove it does not mean the non-existence of such a fact. In this case we have to adopt some other technique or process of finding the truth of those hidden phenomena.

QUESTION: Who should take tantric initiations?
THE DALAI LAMA: The best criteria for receiving initiations, or the minimum qualification for taking the initiation,

is that you should have some understanding or at least some appreciation of the altruistic attitude to achieve Buddhahood for the sake of all sentient beings. Unless you have some appreciation or understanding of *bodhicitta*, or the altruistic intention to achieve Buddhahood for the sake of all sentient beings, it will be impossible for you to cultivate the pure attitude. This is extremely important in tantric practice, where you have to stop the appearance of ordinariness and see everything in a purified way. And the understanding or appreciation of ultimate reality or emptiness is extremely important, particularly in tantric practice. Tantric Buddhist practice involves transforming yourself into a deity, and that is possible only if you're able to absorb filling the ordinariness into the state of ultimate reality or emptiness. So unless you have some understanding or appreciation of ultimate reality or emptiness it is impossible to meditate or cultivate the intent.

QUESTION: What if I find practising two Buddhist Mahayana lineages equally beneficial? I find they complement each other well. Can I practise them both?

THE DALAI LAMA: The Buddhism that flourished in Tibet comprised all the teachings of the Buddha including the Theravadan, Mahayana and Tantra teachings. And within

Mahayana of course there is the practice of both Sutra-
yana and Tantrayana.

In terms of practice, one should start doing the
practice of the higher levels of the teaching only when
one has gained a good understanding or undergone
good practice of the lower levels of the teaching. In
short, all these different levels of the teachings should be
practised by any one individual. In terms of the philosophical tenets, even though we practise all the four
philosophical Buddhist tenets — that is Vaibashika,
Sautantrika, Cittamatra and Madhyamika — we nearly
always study or place emphasis on the practice
of the Mind Only School and the Madhyamika School.
This clearly shows that you should have an understanding of all these lower philosophical schools. Also in
Tibet, in terms of the period of translation of teachings
of the Buddha and of the great Buddhist teachers at
different periods, gradually we came to have what we
call the four Tibetan Buddhist schools of tradition. They
are Sakya, Nyingma, Kagyu and Gelugpa. These all
belong to the Mahayana tradition, and they all practise
the tantric tradition. In fact, they all practise the Anut-
tarayoga tantric tradition. So because they all accept the
Madhyamika philosophical point of view, it is extremely

important for one individual to practise all these four schools of thought without adopting a sectarian attitude. Therefore one can receive different commentaries and initiations belonging to all these four schools of thought.

QUESTION: What benefit do you think Buddhism can have for Australia?

THE DALAI LAMA: I don't know! Of course, generally speaking, Buddhism definitely can make some contribution for some people regarding peace of mind, so that society is transformed and becomes more peaceful and there is more harmony. To that extent it can make a contribution. Then there are Australians who are originally from countries like China or Vietnam which are traditionally Buddhist, so for them to hear the Buddha's teachings is useful.

QUESTION: You spoke of our looking for the transcendental. Can you please explain or elaborate on the nature of the transcendental Buddha mind — that is, is the Buddha that we take refuge in a consciousness or super-consciousness entity? And is it external to ourselves or something internal?

THE DALAI LAMA: When we talk about the mind or the consciousness it has two properties, two qualities — clarity and awareness, or knowledge and knowing the object.

These two properties of the mind are there right from the beginning as a kind of innate, inborn quality. They need not be cultivated through making a new effort.

Even though this is the case, we're unable to cognise or know certain objects because of hindrances or obstructions, as well as a lack of other favourable causes and conditions. The more we accumulate those favourable causes and conditions and remove the obstructions and hindrances, gradually the cognisant power of the mind — the mind being able to know the object, that clarity aspect — becomes stronger and stronger. Through this process we gradually achieve the state of enlightened mind. The contaminations that we have within our mind are temporary; by nature the mind has the quality to cognise or know the object.

The Four Noble Truths

When we say that one who sees dependent arising sees the Dharma, this means gaining a conviction that if we do good we will have good results, and if we do bad we will have bad results. When we're able to see this infallible connection between causes and conditions we'll be able to see the Dharma.

In order to remove suffering, it's extremely important to first identify the suffering of suffering: suffering as something undesirable or unwanted. Once we see the actual nature of suffering and feel disgusted with that, we naturally look for the cause of those sufferings. Suffering is taught in the Four Noble Truths: firstly the truth that suffering exists and secondly, the cause or origin of suffering.

The next step is to make an investigation in which we try to find out whether the causes of suffering can be eliminated. Through this process of research and enquiry, when we finally find that the causes of suffering can be eliminated and that it is possible to achieve a state of total cessation of suffering, we desire to actualise or achieve that state of cessation of, or liberation from, suffering.

So the Third Noble Truth, that of cessation, is taught at this level. Seeing the benefit of achieving cessation, we naturally look towards the path which leads to it. The path leading to the achievement of cessation is taught at the fourth level.

Through reflection, it is extremely important to gain a good understanding about the possibility of achieving such cessation of suffering. This is so, because unless there is a possibility of putting an end to suffering, and unless there is a path which leads to the cessation of suffering, then there's no point in reflecting or meditating on suffering and the cause of suffering.

Some people think that Buddhism is a very pessimistic religion, always asking us to reflect on everything in the nature of suffering. This could be true if we do not have an understanding about the possibility of achieving the true cessation of suffering and the path leading to that.

There are people who ask why we should think and talk about suffering. They say that this world is so beautiful, and we're living in a beautiful, happy world, so why should we think about and meditate on suffering? The only problem with this is that we will not achieve liberation. In order to achieve the high level of happiness and peace of liberation, it is worthwhile to meditate on suffering and to voluntarily undergo some kind of hardship.

Let us take the example of our ordinary daily life. In order to achieve a certain amount of wealth, peace and happiness in the latter part of life, we work very hard at the beginning of life. We work so hard that we might forget to sleep and eat. We're doing so because we have an objective, which is to achieve some kind of long-lasting happiness in the latter part of life.

Similarly, when we engage in Buddhist practice in order to achieve the higher state of happiness of liberation or enlightenment, it is extremely worthwhile to undergo certain temporary hardships. In order to enjoy a certain calmness, relaxation and happiness later in life, we are ready to sacrifice certain moments of relaxation or peace, temporarily.

When we talk about meditating on true suffering, we're speaking about the basic nature of our reality and existence. Our present state within the cyclic existence of life is very much controlled by contaminated actions and delusions. This kind of existence is called suffering. So when we talk about meditating on suffering we have to meditate on this basic nature of our psycho-physical existence.

To explain the nature of suffering a little more, first of all we have what we call the suffering of suffering. This does not necessarily refer to feeling alone, but to the state of encountering numerous sufferings within cyclic existence. These are the categories of suffering which we normally identify and recognise as suffering.

We also encounter the second level of suffering, which is called the suffering of change. At this level we have experiences of suffering like engaging in certain activities which we tend to think will bring us a lot of happiness, peace and so forth. And we may get peace and happiness temporarily; but if we engage in and rely on that state of peace and happiness for a longer time, it begins to diminish and gradually it will change into suffering.

The third category of suffering is called pervasive compositional suffering. This refers to the fact that something is wrong with the very nature of our psycho-physical existence. In our ordinary life we all know that we encounter the sufferings of old age, sickness, death and birth. In fact, there are people who do not want to even hear the word 'death'. This clearly indicates that these are the sufferings we do not want. In short, our life starts with suffering, the suffering of birth, and our life comes to an end with suffering, the suffering of death. In between these two sufferings we also have the suffering of old age, of sickness, of encountering things we don't want or not encountering things we want. In this way, we encounter numerous sufferings.

We encounter all these sufferings because we have taken part in this cyclic existence. Our very existence at the time of birth is suffering, because we have not taken birth out of compassion. We have taken birth within cyclic existence propelled or projected by the strong force of our contaminated actions and delusions. This is why we encounter suffering. It is the law of nature that whatever is caused by forces and conditions will finally disintegrate and come to an end.

The true nature of reality

We all desire happiness and do not want suffering and this is a kind of innate quality that we have within us. But if we reflect carefully we see that even though we want happiness we always tend to engage in a way of life or of thinking that accumulates more negative activities that lead to suffering. And even though we do not want suffering, we always tend to run after suffering. In other words, we always tend to do what should not be done, and we do not do what should be done. So we engage in a perverse way of life. If we reflect carefully on the cause of this, we'll be able to find out that the cause of this negative way of life, engaging in wrong actions and thinking is ignorance.

Of course, when we talk about ignorance there could be countless levels and varieties of ignorance. But we're talking here about fundamental ignorance or fundamental confusion, which actually is a wrong state of consciousness. It does not have a valid foundation, it is unreasonable, and it is a mistaken state of consciousness which sees things as having independent or inherent existence. It's because of this fundamental ignorance that we encounter all the negativities of life.

There are grosser levels of ignorance and subtle levels of

ignorance. In fact, ignorance means a state of mind which wrongly understands or wrongly grasps at the truth. It grasps at the opposite of ultimate reality. This is its nature.

When we give a general definition of ignorance, we can say that ignorance is a state of mind which is unable to distinguish between what is to be practised and what is to be given up. This general explanation of the meaning of ignorance can be accepted by all the four Buddhist philosophical tenets.

But if we give a more profound explanation of ignorance by saying that ignorance is a state of mind which wrongly grasps at the nature of ultimate reality, the explanations will be different because the four Buddhist schools of thought have different interpretations of the meaning of ultimate reality.

If we explain the meaning of ignorance in accordance with the highest school of thought, which is the Prasangika-Madhyamika or Middle-Way School, ignorance actually refers to the state of mind which wrongly sees all phenomena as having independent or inherent existence, or existence from their own side. Such a state of mind is ignorant because the ultimate nature of all phenomena is that they have a dependent, relative nature.

Therefore, when we talk about ignorance it is extremely important for us to understand and realise that this ignorance actually means having a strong grasping to ourselves and all phenomena. Because of this ignorance, we tend to see ourselves as something absolutely independent and existing from our own side. Based on this solid grasping of the 'I', we cultivate a strong attachment to ourselves, and this view of the ignorant mind brings problems, brings trouble.

It is important for us to discriminate here that when we say we should not cultivate a strong attachment to ourselves, this does not mean that we should ignore ourselves. There's nothing wrong in taking care of ourselves, in loving ourselves, in showing compassion to ourselves. What we're objecting to here is cultivating a strong attachment based on ignorance. Because when we have this strong grasping to ourselves and cultivate attachment and so forth, we tend to see ourselves as the most important, and the rest of the sentient beings as something we should not care about.

In fact, in one of the texts it clearly says that when we have this strong self-grasping within, we make a boundary line, or demarcation, saying that: 'These are my side and these are the side of other people.' Once we make this demarcation, we cultivate attachment to those nearer to us, those that we love, and hatred and anger towards those we have categorised as belonging to others. That induces the arising of many more afflictive emotions, which then cultivate further contaminated actions or negative karma. And it is in this way that we wander aimlessly within cyclic existence.

If we're able to see that ignorance is the root cause of all these problems, we can see the importance of getting rid of such an ignorant disturbed state of mind. As long as we're under the power and control of this ignorant state of mind there's no opportunity for us to have any kind of long-lasting peace and happiness.

It's important for us to realise that the enemies are not outside. The real enemy, in fact, the sworn enemy, is ignorance ...

As practitioners, it is important for us to realise that this condition or state of existence is within cyclic existence. This is what is known as pervasive compositional suffering. It is extremely important to realise and gain conviction in the fact that as long as we have this ignorance residing peacefully within our mind we will never have the occasion to achieve liberation and a permanent state of happiness. It's important for us to realise that the enemies are not outside. The real enemy, in fact, the sworn enemy, is ignorance, which we need to combat and get rid of if we really want to put an end to cyclic existence and suffering.

This ignorance has brought us countless problems in our past lives. And today we're encountering numerous sufferings because of this ignorance, which is residing peacefully within our mind. If we continue with this way of life, it is definite that in future lives also we will endlessly encounter suffering.

Once that dominant ignorance is overthrown and we have overcome the inner enemy, this is salvation. If we reflect carefully in this way, we will be able to understand and gain conviction of how destructive, negative and horrible these afflictive emotions are.

There are countless classes of afflictive emotions, but we can summarise the major ones in two ways. On the one hand we have attachment, which arises basically because of our wrong way of looking at things. Because of our wrong conceptual thought, we tend to see objects as extremely pleasant, attractive and interesting. There may be some attractive and interesting aspect within the object, but when we cultivate such a negative afflictive emotion like that of attachment, we tend to see something more than what is there. We tend to see the object as one hundred per cent attractive, interesting and pleasant, and based on that we cultivate a very strong negative attachment.

In the case of something that we do not want, we tend to see the object as completely disgusting and horrible. We do not see any positive or good points in that object, and we try to distance ourselves from it. Because of such a mental attitude we cultivate a strong hatred and anger towards such an object.

There is a clear indication of how these wrong negative conceptual thoughts exaggerate the object of reality and, based on that, how they cultivate attachment and anger. When we cultivate attachment towards an object, we tend not to see any defects or faults in it. But as soon as a certain change of circumstance or situation occurs and we find some fault within that particular object, suddenly our whole attitude changes and we see the same object as negative, horrible and bad.

This clearly indicates that what we have seen as one hundred per cent positive and what we have seen as one hundred per cent negative is not an objective reality but mental fabrication. If it had been reality, under all situations and circumstances the object should be one hundred per cent negative or one hundred per cent positive. But this is not the case. It changes because of a change in our own mental attitude, and is based on the exaggeration that our mind has made around that particular object.

It is crucial to remember that when it comes to the cultivation or experiencing of positive qualities such as loving kindness, compassion, altruism and so forth, these should of course be analysed by intellectual thought; when through that process we gain some feeling at an emotional level, at that time we should experience it and leave it at that emotional level. We should not engage in any further intellectual exercise. But when it comes to the arousal of the negative afflictive emotions, we should not give them an opportunity to intrude at an emotional level. Rather, we should try to distinguish and judge the different natures of these afflictive emotions through discriminative intelligence.

In other words, I think that we must try to investigate the negative things more objectively, without a sense of involvement. Then, in regard to the positive things, make a thorough investigation not only objectively, but also with a sense of involvement. That I think can be done. At the intellectual level, make a clear sort of distinction, such as 'this is harmful, this is bad', then take countermeasures for these things but without negative emotions. But for the positive things, we need not only intellectual distinction but also a sense of involvement. If we remain purely objective with positive things, then we become without feeling — cold like a computer. That's not good.

In addition to the basic dominant afflictive emotions of attachment and hatred, there are many other afflictive emotions that are induced by such negative states of mind as jealousy, covetousness and so forth.

It's important to distinguish the meaning of the term 'desire', because it can have a positive and a negative connotation. For example, certain texts explain that desire and craving are the negative emotions which bind within cyclic existence.

Such texts explain desire as something that should be discarded and given up. But at the same time it's important to understand that not all desires are negative. There are positive desires and there are also negative desires. Those desires that bind us within cyclic existence are negative afflictive emotions; these are something that we do not want, something that should be given up.

But there are also positive desires, like the desire to achieve Buddhahood, and the desire to cultivate bodhicitta or altruism within our mind. These positive desires must be cultivated. So it is important to distinguish the different levels of desire.

There could be two categories in the case of anger also. One is motivated by a compassionate attitude, a mind wishing to benefit other sentient beings. And there is anger which is motivated by a wish to harm other sentient beings.

With doubt there could also be two categories. One is what we call afflictive doubt, which is a negative afflictive emotion and something we must not cultivate. Then there could also be a positive kind of doubt which is helpful; particularly in Buddhism when we talk about following a teaching based on reason and logic. Such reason and logic could be cultivated by first remaining sceptical and not coming to a conclusion hurriedly without seeing the reason and the logic.

In the *Abhisamayalamkara* (*Ornament of Realisation*) by Maitreya, two categories of followers of that text are explained: the blunt student and the sharp student. Blunt students are those who simply follow that particular text out of devotion. The second category of followers of that text are students with a sharp mental faculty. These students would not follow that particular teaching out of devotion but would first examine it, remain sceptical and have doubt about its authenticity. After engaging in study, reflection and meditation, once these students find that the teaching is reasonable and logical, only then would they follow it. So, in that particular text, the process of cultivating faith based on reason and logic is highly praised. It's extremely important to have such a kind of positive doubt.

In the case of the cultivation of faith, there could be one-pointed faith which is a result of thorough examination, study, meditation and reflection. Such a kind of one-pointed faith is extremely beneficial in Buddhist practice. There could be another kind of one-pointed faith, however, which is totally derived from devotion and not from study, logical reasoning and so forth. Such one-pointed faith might prove quite dangerous, because the student could be guided to all kinds of different levels of teaching without understanding what he or she is following. That might prove quite risky to such a practitioner.

Even in the case of a very strong afflictive emotion such

as hatred, there could be two categories. Of course, if we have hatred for some other sentient beings, that is totally negative and inappropriate. It is always negative. But why can't we have hatred towards our afflictive emotions?

In the case of feelings of egotism, there again could be two categories. One is the negative kind of egotism in which we tend to think of ourselves as supreme and wonderful; because of this strong negative sense of self, we tend to completely ignore the welfare and happiness of other sentient beings. Such negative egotism or egotistic feeling is wrong and should be discarded.

But there could be another, positive egotism or egotistic feeling. For example, we can think that we have been born as a human being, we have capacity and intelligence. We can do Dharma practice. We can help other sentient beings and achieve Buddhahood. We will work very hard to liberate all sentient beings and to remove their sufferings. Such strong positive egotism is extremely useful in practice.

Therefore, included in the term 'emotion' there are so many different levels that we must distinguish carefully. A mental attitude or emotion could be inappropriate and negative in a certain situation, but appropriate and useful in a different situation.

Let us take the example of the one-pointed decision to

become liberated from cyclic existence. In this case, a one-pointed desire to achieve liberation is perfectly suitable for a person whose capacity is only to achieve liberation and who does not have the capacity to achieve higher spiritual practices like the cultivation of altruism, to achieve enlightenment for the sake of all sentient beings.

But such a one-pointed desire just to achieve liberation for oneself is inappropriate for a person who has the higher capacity to practise the cultivation of altruism to achieve enlightenment for the sake of all sentient beings. Because the cultivation of altruism is more beneficial and profound, it is a more useful practice than the achievement of liberation just for oneself.

Karma

Based on our afflictive emotions, we accumulate countless varieties of contaminated actions or karma. Again there are countless varieties of karma. Basically, the term 'karma' or 'action' can be related to the natural process of the law of phenomena, the law of causality. But here when we talk about karma, we're referring to a particular action accumulated by sentient beings that affects the experience of happiness and suffering of other sentient beings, based on a certain motivation.

From the Buddhist point of view, if a particular practice

becomes a strong counterforce in removing the negative afflictive emotions, that could be termed a genuine practice. On the
other hand, those practices that do not act as a counterforce, or
that do not combat the negative afflictive emotions, are not
genuine Dharma or genuine practice.

So whether we are practising actual, good Dharma or not
depends upon whether that practice becomes a counterforce in
removing the afflictive emotions or not. In order to combat,
oppose and eliminate the afflictive emotions or delusions, it
is extremely important first of all to identify the nature or
characteristics and the destructiveness of the afflictive emotion.
Unless we can identify these characteristics there is no way to
oppose and combat them. This is similar to the ordinary way:
if we are to fight our enemy it is crucial to first identify the
enemy's strength, power and location. Only after identifying
these characteristics can we prepare ourselves to combat the
enemy.

As we have discussed, these afflictive emotions arise in
conjunction with our basic mind, in the form of various levels
of mental factors. Of course, there are countless varieties of
negative afflictive emotions and, therefore, it is extremely
important first of all for us to identify all their different natures
and varieties. It is also extremely important to maintain mindfulness and conscientiousness always, which means to know when

these afflictive emotions arise, to know how destructive they are, and not to give them the chance to gain control over us.

It is so important that we do not give the afflictive emotions the chance to arise because when they do arise and our mind is controlled and overpowered by them, we are unable to control ourselves. Because of the influence of these afflictive emotions, we express ourselves negatively in a physical, verbal or mental way, which leads us to accumulate strong negative contaminated karma or actions.

> We call actions virtuous because
> when we engage in them, they result
> in happiness.

In terms of karma or action, we can speak principally about virtuous action and non-virtuous action. Virtuous action refers to those positive levels of action that when engaged in bring peace resulting in long-lasting happiness. Non-virtuous actions are those that result in or lead to experiencing long-lasting suffering and problems. When we talk about virtuous action and non-virtuous action, this is not something we identify because Buddha said they are virtuous and non-virtuous. We call actions virtuous because when we engage in them, they result in happiness. What we want is happiness. What we do not want is suffering, so when a certain negative way of life or certain negative actions are engaged in, they lead to the experience of suffering. So these are called non-virtuous actions.

When we talk about afflictive emotions or delusions, these are states of mind which leave us completely disturbed and unhappy, and our mind completely agitated. That is the function, or the destructive nature of the afflictive emotions or delusions. Let us take the example of the arousal of strong hatred. When that negative afflictive emotion of hatred arises within our mind, at that very moment our mind gets completely disturbed and agitated. Because of that, we might react and express ourselves very negatively. We might fight other people or go to war and so forth. In this way, we also destroy the happiness of other people. Hatred not only brings disturbance within our mind and the minds of other people, but can destroy the peace and happiness of the whole atmosphere. When there is a strong influence of hatred and anger, even birds or animals in that environment would not be able to experience joy. In fact, they would feel upset and disturbed. That's the negative result of such afflictive emotions.

As soon as we have harmed the other person, the actual manifested actions cease to function. While we are engaging in the process of accumulating that particular action, it leaves an imprint on the continuity of the mind (or the continuum of the mind, or the stream of the 'I' or the self). Normally, the philosophical tenets explain that when we refer to the continuity of the mind, this acts as a temporary basis for carrying the imprints. It is actually the continuity of the self or the 'I' that acts as the long-term basis for carrying the positive or negative imprint — the mere 'I'.

So the continuity of that mere 'I' flows on and carries the imprints. Because of that, in subsequent lives that same continuity experiences the result of the negative karma that the preceding continuity of the 'I' has accumulated. In this way, we can clearly see that the accumulation of negative karma does not only lead to experiencing a temporary negative result, but it leads to long-lasting negative results, to long-lasting sufferings.

We could also categorise karma into three levels. One is called the karma that leads to experiencing the result in this very life. This kind of karma is actually a very powerful and strong kind of karma, and because of the accumulation of that strong karma the result could be experienced in this very life. For example, if we have accumulated a very strong negative karma at the beginning of our lives, we will experience the result in the later part of our lives.

In the second category of karma, we do not experience the results in this life, but in the immediate next life. Then there is a third category of karma, whose results we will not experience in this life or in the immediate next life but after many subsequent lives or after the immediate next life.

Now the question is, how is the link made between this life and the next life? Let us take the example of a human being. We possess a very gross physical body and at the time of death the body and mind get disconnected. The mind leaves the gross physical body behind as it is put in fire or buried or thrown in water or whatever; the body is lost and the mind travels to the next life. When we speak about a person, a being or a sentient being, it should be understood in terms of having experience or feelings of happiness and suffering. It cannot be determined simply from the point of view of having a life, because even non-sentient beings like flowers also have a life; they also have a duration in which they come into existence and in which they finally come to an end.

But at the same time, some people say that some of these flowers have a kind of feeling. If we treat them properly they grow well, and if we treat them negatively they do not grow well and they die out. It is important to make further investigation of this. When we try to differentiate between sentient beings and non-sentient beings, it should be done from the point of view of whether they possess mind or consciousness or not. Whatever possesses mind and consciousness is a sentient being, while those that do not possess mind or feelings are non-sentient beings, even though they have a life.

What do we mean by 'mind'? What is it? Properly

speaking, we have what we call the five sense consciousnesses and the sixth which is the mental consciousness. But basically when we talk about mind or consciousness, we are actually referring to the sixth consciousness, that is the mental consciousness. There are countless categories within mental consciousness, so we should not misunderstand by thinking that mental consciousness is just one single identity. There are virtuous states of mind, non-virtuous states of mind, grosser levels of mental consciousness, subtler levels of mental consciousness and so forth.

It is from this point of view that in Buddhism we do not accept a soul because the word 'soul' has the connotation of a single, permanent, partless identity. Because this meaning of a soul is quite similar to the definition of a person as explained in some ancient non-Buddhist theosophical thought — in which the person is identified as something single, solitary, partless and permanent — likewise the proponents of the soul also say that the soul is something single, partless and permanent; so therefore Buddhists refute such an idea.

Emptiness

In one of Nagarjuna's texts, called *Fundamental Wisdom*, he says that liberation is a state of cessation of contaminated actions and delusions, and that contaminated actions arise from delusions; delusions arise from wrong conceptual thought, and wrong conceptual thought arises from true grasping or ignorance. Nagarjuna further says that the counterforce or the positive opposing factor by which we can get rid of ignorance or self-grasping is emptiness. There is also a second version, which says that ignorance and self-grasping cease to exist in the nature of emptiness.

So in the case of the first version, that the ignorance of true grasping can be eliminated by emptiness, this means that when we use the wisdom realising emptiness or understanding ultimate reality, we can eliminate the wrong conception of reality that is ignorance or true grasping. So that is one way of removing the ignorance.

The second version states that the self-grasping or ignorance ceases to exist in the nature of emptiness. This means that once we realise the ultimate nature or reality of our mind, this ignorance or self-grasping ceases to arise and therefore ceases to exist in that very nature.

Now, what is emptiness? Emptiness does not refer to nothingness. You may ask, if it is not equal to nothingness then what do we mean by emptiness? Emptiness actually refers to a state of existence which is different from the way we tend to see existent phenomena. This is important to understand. Normally, we get into trouble because we tend to cling and grasp when things appear to us. We are unable to see the actual nature or reality of phenomena and are completely deceived by their appearance. When we are too deceived, or when we are too attracted to such appearances of phenomena, based on that we tend to exaggerate them and see the extreme side of that reality. Because of that, we cultivate attachment, anger and other conceptual thoughts which lead to suffering.

> ... emptiness actually means lack of
> inherent or independent existence.

So when we talk about emptiness we are saying that things do not have an existence as they seem to exist to our ordinary level of mind. Therefore, emptiness actually means lack of inherent or independent existence. When we see something, we tend to see that object, whether external or internal, as having an independent existence from its own side. Because of this way of thinking about independent existence, we see something solid and long-lasting, and based on that we cultivate attachment and so forth. Through that we get into trouble. So it is extremely important to realise that things do not have such an independent existence.

Again in *Fundamental Wisdom* by Nagarjuna, he states that when we talk about emptiness it actually refers to the dependent nature of a particular phenomenon. Because of that dependent nature it lacks inherent existence, and because of that

lack of inherent existence it is something which is merely des-
ignated by conceptual thought as having a name and so forth.
Apart from that designation and apart from that dependent
nature, there is no phenomenon which exists from its own side.

Now, let us examine how things appear to us. When a
particular object appears to us, we tend to cling by thinking
that it has an objective existence from its own side, which is
completely independent of any other causes and conditions. If
it has an objective existence as it appears to us, then we should
be able to find that objective existence if we investigate and
analyse it. The more we analyse and investigate, the more the
object should become clear. In modern quantum physics also
— even though the physicists' field of experiment, of course,
is a physical thing — when they experiment and investigate a
physical object, they state that the more and more they analyse
and investigate to find that particular physical object, they do
not find it, it just disappears. Therefore, some modern physicists
are reluctant to use the word 'reality', because when they investigate and analyse, they do not find it.

When we realise that things do not have independent
existence as they appear to us, the advantage of such a realisation
is that the next time that things appear to us as something very
attractive or very negative, at that point we will be able to
realise that this particular object is an illusion. Even though it

appears to us as very negative, this again is false and an illusion. These things do not have independent existence as they appear to us. With that kind of realisation we are able to weaken and reduce the strength and arousal of negative afflictive emotions such as attachment, hatred and so forth.

Through study we gain some understanding or idea about the possibility of achieving a state of liberation from cyclic existence. Even though we have not actualised such a state of liberation, because we have some understanding of the possibility we may be encouraged to meditate on emptiness.

When you look around at the sentient beings surrounding yourself, if you analyse and watch the kind of mental attitude you adopt towards these sentient-being friends you will find that you have categorised them. You have treated some of these sentient beings very dearly and very closely, thinking that they are your friends and relatives. And then you have another section of sentient beings towards whom you have a very negative attitude; treating them as your enemies, as something very bad and bringing harm upon them. You have also a section of sentient beings towards whom you have no particular interest; you do not like them or hate them, you have a neutral stand towards them. Because of this biased mental attitude you have brought a lot of harm within yourself and upon the rest of the sentient beings.

Now, compare this wrong mental attitude that you have with that of the mental attitude of the Buddhas. When the Buddhas and Bodhisattvas look towards these sentient beings, they do not adopt a biased mental attitude because they see all sentient beings as their friends, as their very close relatives and friends. They do not discriminate towards these sentient beings. And because of the wrong attitude that you have adopted you have brought a lot of harm and suffering upon the rest of the sentient beings, and thereby upon yourself also. If you see it in this way, you will clearly recognise what a foolish and short-sighted way of life you have led. And through that recognition you should make a promise, make a commitment, deciding that henceforth you will follow the wonderful example of Shakya-muni Buddha and discard this sectarian view or discriminative way of looking at sentient beings.

So here you should think: 'Today, fortunately, I have access to this wonderful opportunity of practising and listening to the Buddhadharma, and because of listening to the teachings of the Buddha and following his example my eyes have been opened. Now I have gained some kind of discriminative awareness. I am able to distinguish what is to be practised and what is to be given up. I am able to distinguish what is positive and what is negative, and therefore I must not waste this wonderful opportunity. I will follow the wonderful example of Shakyamuni Buddha.'

CHAPTER FOUR

THE PATH TO HAPPINESS:
An explanation of the teachings and initiations

In Australia and New Zealand in 2002, the Dalai Lama will give a range of teachings. This chapter contains an explanation of some of these teachings such as: the Four Noble Truths, the *Eight Verses of Thought Transformation*, Atisha's *Lamp for the Path to Enlightenment*, and brief explanations about the Chenrezig and White Tara initiations.

As the Dalai Lama explains in Chapter Three, an understanding of the Four Noble Truths is essential. These fundamental teachings of the Buddha are necessary for all those starting out on the path to true happiness. At every stage we need to remind ourselves of these foundations, otherwise we may fall prey to the endless distractions around us and lose sight of the basic unsatisfactoriness of our existence. The Buddha taught that the attainment of a calm, happy and relaxed mind is our birthright. It is a state of lasting happiness that we all desire, and which is possible to attain. But we must begin by facing the truth of suffering as fundamental to our existence. Once that has been acknowledged and explained in terms of its causes, we can begin to appreciate and move towards the ending of suffering and the path that takes us there. This is the essence of the Four Noble Truths.

The Four Noble Truths

When the historic Buddha, Prince Gautama Siddhartha, finally attained enlightenment, after years of trying to get to the heart of what it is to be human, he was speechless. There was nothing he could say, nothing to say.

He had awoken by his own efforts. He had many teachers and fellow meditators along the way, but none had been able to show or lead him to full awakening. He had to do it by himself. Having completely awoken, he immediately realised that anyone who seeks happiness must do the same, or remain trapped in self-defeating strategies.

The Buddha's awakening to the insubstantiality of everything that we usually take seriously and literally was the basis of liberation. From that moment on he was not trapped in the endless cycle of suffering.

He was free, but all around him people were going round in circles, seeking happiness here, there and everywhere, and tripping themselves up. His awakening made him much more sensitive to others, more attuned, more engaged with them. Far from becoming self-absorbed, he found that to awaken is to be more receptive, observant and connected. He saw that others were in pain, sometimes more than they realised, as they went about their daily lives, always hoping things would turn out right.

So intense was the Buddha's desire to help people past their pain that he found a way to convey his realisations. Just hearing the teachings is not enlightenment, it is simply pointing the way to enlightenment. The words he chose to describe the path were simple, deliberately so, in order to avoid confusion.

The Buddha's very first teaching after he attained enlightenment is known as the 'Teaching on the Four Noble Truths'.

The First Noble Truth
The truth of suffering

A simple, honest observation of our own experience of life is that it is basically dissatisfying. At first we might think that there are highs and lows in life, moments when everything falls apart, which are balanced by other times when life is great. But, in the first of his many teachings, the Buddha invited us to look more closely, to observe from moment to moment the actual nature of our experience.

He found that we constantly live through a cycle of roller-coaster emotions. That unpredictable cycle is a source of anxiety in itself. We seldom know what is going to happen next. Our desire for certainty and predictability is strong. Modern life requires us to feel in control, and all our new technologies give us the powerful illusion that we have almost gained control over our circumstances. But when we look more closely, we see that our lives are governed by hope and fear. We swing between these two constantly and hope things will improve. We hope that whatever is good shall last and whatever is unpleasant will disappear. Conversely, we fear that what's good won't last or that we will be stuck in a bad situation forever. We are imprisoned. If we look very closely, we find that even the most sublime or passionate moments are often tinged with this fear: will it last?

This First Noble Truth encourages us to watch our experience, unsentimentally, and observe the plunging and soaring turnover of emotions. It invites us also to observe the times when nothing much seems to happen, so that we can fully taste the flavour of those seemingly neutral times, but even these seem to have a slightly negative tone; a tendency to turn away, to close off and not look too closely at the truth of our experience.

The Buddha taught this First Noble Truth as an invitation

to examine the taste of reality in our experience. Even if your life is wonderful compared to others, your circumstances can change. You may believe that other people are more fortunate than yourself, but they are experiencing dissatisfaction also. Perhaps the suffering in the mind of a rich person can be as intense as that of a beggar.

The Dalai Lama explains it this way:

'If you compare rich and poor people, it often seems that the people who have nothing are in fact those with the least worries. As for the rich, while some wealthy people know how to use their wealth intelligently, others do not, and we can see to what degree they are constantly anxious and tormented, torn between hope and doubt, even if they seem to be successful in everything.'[1]

The Buddha didn't say life is grim, just that it is change-able and unpredictable. As long as we want it to be known, safe, predictable and under control, we are going to be disappointed. If we look at our lives honestly, we see that we are prey to a lot of stress and anxiety.

The Second Noble Truth
Suffering has a cause

Just to say that life is unsatisfactory is not a help. We must go on and identify precisely the single cause of our dissatisfaction.

At first, what the Buddha identified as the cause may

seem odd. He said that our suffering is due to making ourselves the centre of everything. It comes about through a narrow, ingrained, obsessive, habitual focus on 'me'.

From the Buddha's point of view, we are forever re-inventing ourselves, telling ourselves stories about who we are, what we do and don't do, how we feel towards this person and that, remembering and reliving the past and anticipating the future. Our lives become a big production, like a feature-length film or a soap opera, and it takes us a lot of effort to hang onto all the ideas we have about who we are.

Up to a point, we may agree that we can get too bound up in ourselves, too self-absorbed, never making enough room for others. Yet, from a Buddhist point of view, a healthy sense of self is fine, even necessary as a basic tool for getting on with the practicalities of life.

Ego or self is not a problem, but the value we place on it is. If our ego is a servant, keeping track of things, we are fine. But if ego takes over, we have a problem. When everything we do has to serve ego, prop up a brittle sense of self and feed our ego's insatiable demand for reassurance in an unpredictable world, we have a problem. The Buddha taught that the cause of suffering is self-centredness. That's when we give ego the reins, surrendering to its claim to be the author of our lives.

An egocentric person uses strategies for life, seeking

advantages, on the alert to score a win, even if someone else loses. Saying that this approach is wrong is not a moral commandment from on high, but a practical observation that it just doesn't work. Meditation invites us to check whether putting ourselves first gets a result. Is there a pattern? Do we set ourselves up to fail?

Acknowledging the cause of suffering reduces self-cherishing. Until now me, myself and I have come first and everyone else a distant second. The alternative is to relax, be a bit more spacious and make room for others; to acknowledge that they just want happiness too, and are struggling to overcome dissatisfaction. The things we have in common are far more important than our differences.

The Third Noble Truth
The cessation of suffering

The Buddha then taught a revolutionary truth: it is possible to live a calm life of equanimity, happiness and joy, in which dissatisfaction no longer exists in the mind. This is a real alternative to being the victim of our own confusions, anxieties, hopes, fears and fixations.

A classic Buddhist image is to see the world as covered in nasty prickly thorns. To walk barefoot is to risk painful wounds. What can we do? We could mount a huge project to cover the world with leather, creating a soft and safe surface to walk on, or we can cover our feet with leather and be safe.

A pair of shoes is a much simpler answer than trying to make the whole world safe. No political leader throughout history has succeeded in making the world safe, but if we change our minds, even if it's dangerous out there, we still have an inner freedom to choose how to respond. The mind that has made a fundamental change in perspective is no longer a slave to habit. It generates its own happiness, and is not dependent on an unending struggle to manipulate external conditions.

The Buddha is an embodied example of the joy of a changed mind. In the stories of his life he dealt with everyone in the same open, happy way. One person might praise him lavishly, another hate him and even plan to kill him, yet he treated them both with the same calm, direct equanimity.

The Dalai Lama is an example for us of the cessation of suffering. Raised to be a king of both the secular and sacred realms of an entire nation, he lost everything a powerful person can lose: his nation, his homeland, his monasteries and the heritage of a great civilisation. Martin Scorsese's 1997 film *Kundun* describes this intimately. Yet, despite this series of disasters, the Dalai Lama never lost his inner equanimity and happiness, or sank into depression. The exiled Dalai Lama, at the lowest point in his life, makes it clear that he is angry with no one. He remains responsible for his own happiness, even in the most extreme situations.

The Fourth Noble Truth
The path to the cessation of suffering

This is a new beginning. If dissatisfaction, anxiety and frustration routinely trip us up, and take the edge off even the best times; and if there is a way to exist beyond such frustration, we need it. There is, in fact, a well tested way of moving from chronic dissatisfaction to happiness; this is the path of Buddhist meditation practice.

To profess an answer to frustration is to offer an ending. Yet the Fourth Noble Truth is also the gateway to a constellation of Buddhist methods for transforming the mind and opening the heart. The path is not one neat package. Buddhism offers many methods, depending on individual aptitude, strength of motivation, personality and disposition.

All methods share a common basis, which is to widen our perspective. We discover that we are not our thoughts. We gradually let go of the habit of thinking too much. We loosen the grip of obsessively focusing on 'me' to the exclusion of the bigger picture. We drop much of the baggage we carry. All Buddhist practices reframe the emotions and thoughts that dominate our habit-bound minds, until we discover that they are only waves on the surface of a vast ocean. Who better than the Dalai Lama to help us recognise our fixations in a much wider perspective?

The Buddhist path to the cessation of dissatisfaction and suffering uses the mind to train the mind. In the modern material world knowledge is power. While the modern world places a high value on information and knowledge, it is strangely out of touch when it comes to wisdom — which should be what all our knowledge leads to. Wisdom is profound insight not just into how everything exists, but what it is to be human. All Buddhist methods lead towards that insight, not as an intellectual theory but as a real experience achieved through disciplined effort by the practitioner.

By discovering the nature of the material world, and of the mind, we discover the vast creative, communicative and responsive capabilities of the mind. The cessation of suffering is not a negation, erasing something negative. It opens us to a much more fluid, spontaneous, generous and compassionate way of living. But it's not easy. It goes against the grain of everything we have set up as our personal strategies for life. The modern world encourages us to create strategies to prepare us to live rather than just living. By comparison the Buddhist path can seem too simple, as though we run the risk that others will take advantage of us if we don't keep our guard up. The only way to find out is to try it, and see what happens.

Often it's a great relief to be able to drop some of the accumulated baggage of the constructed self and get on with the next step, the next breath. It can be a great relief not to be so calculating, and to trust ourselves instead, by being open and honest. Above all, it makes life much lighter if we no longer worry about how we appear to others. The Buddhist path is one of inner stability and strength, trust and confidence.

Some of the Buddhist methods provide step-by-step training of the mind, so that our self-defeating habits are gradually replaced by more wholesome habits. As confidence and mental stability grow, other paths to happiness are more direct. They constitute the path to the cessation of suffering, and open the door to a full awakening.

Eight Verses of Thought Transformation

These eight concise verses by Langri Tangpa provide us with sound practical advice for happiness in daily life. Distilled from the experience of deeply committed meditators one thousand years ago, who awoke to their true condition, some of what they offer may surprise you. They often contradict what we think of as the causes of personal happiness. What they are offering is a longer-term, more reliable kind of happiness which comes not from external conditions but from within, and whose touchstone is putting others, not the self, centre stage in our lives.

When this collection of wise sayings was composed, Buddhism was still somewhat new to Tibet but had been practised for 1500 years in India, its birthland. These gems of wisdom were collected by Atisha, then by Langri Tangpa and, later, Geshe Chekawa Yeshe Dorje. The first of these great teachers was born in 982, and the last died in 1175. The Dalai Lama has chosen the *Eight Verses of Thought Transformation* as the text for his principal teaching in New Zealand in 2002. They speak to us with simplicity and clarity, across the gulf of time and space.

The brevity of these verses is their strength. Once they are understood, they are easily memorised and can be recalled at moments in daily life when a fresh approach is needed. Compressing the entire Tibetan mind-training approach into eight verses could make them seem uncompromising and blunt, but they help us generate true loving kindness. As the Dalai Lama often says, all religions teach compassion. This is not unique to Buddhism. But in these eight verses there is a distinctively Buddhist approach to how compassion arises.

From a Buddhist perspective, compassion is unconditional. If I need you to respond to my compassion and tell me how wonderful I am, that is conditional. If I need you to respond at all, heed my advice or mend your ways, that is conditional too. If I have compassion for everyone in a situation I can relate to but still see others less familiar to me as beyond my compassion, that is at best conditional.

Loving kindness and compassion can be consciously learned and deliberately generated, but they can also arise spontaneously and naturally without so much strenuous effort. Compassion is not a moral duty or a commandment, but a natural capability that surfaces when we clear away self-centredness.

Genuine compassion is vigorous and energetic, not just a sentiment. Compassion is not pity, nor a smothering of pain so that everyone feels good.

The focus of these verses is not on rushing into changing the world, but on changing the self. That's why the root text calls itself 'thought transformation'. The proof of whether these slogans are effective or not is whether the practitioner sees reality differently as a result of using the slogans in daily life. These verses are tools of training. When put into practice, they can turn our lives around as they have done for thousands of meditators over the past thousand years.

The *Eight Verses* train us to change course. It's not easy

going against a lifetime habit of putting ourselves first. It may seem unnatural to hand victory to others, be grateful to everyone, to change our attitude and yet remain natural. But when we use these tools of training, we discover that the immediate beneficiary is not others out there, but me. It's a relief to drop the obsessive preoccupation with self, the striving to be a unique individual making our statement. What these verses ask of us is not a superhuman effort to be more moral and dutiful than ever, but to relax and let there be space to connect simply with others.

As a great lama of recent times, Chogyam Trungpa Rinpoche, says: 'This practice opens up a greater field of tenderness and strength, so that our actions are based on appreciation rather than the ongoing cycle of hope and fear.'[2] We appreciate what is, rather than get stuck about what could have been or should be. We appreciate reality as it presents itself, even when it shocks us.

When we start to practise these verses in daily life, we find they undo the self-centredness, purify the mind's cluttered habits and process anew what we have come to take for granted. They soften us from within and challenge our strictly personal quest for happiness.

With a determination to accomplish
The highest welfare of all sentient beings
Who surpass even a wish-granting jewel,
I will learn to hold them supremely dear.

The Dalai Lama explains this verse as follows:

'Other sentient beings are really the principal source of all our experiences of joy, happiness, and prosperity, and not only in terms of our day-to-day dealings with people. All the desirable experiences that we cherish or aspire to attain are dependent upon co-operation and interaction with other sentient beings. It is an obvious fact.

'Similarly, from the point of view of a practitioner on the path, many of the high levels of realisation that you gain and the progress you make on your spiritual journey are dependent upon co-operation and interaction with other sentient beings. Furthermore, in the resultant state of Buddhahood, the truly compassionate activities of a Buddha can come about spontaneously without any effort only in relation to sentient beings, because they are the recipients and beneficiaries of those enlightened activities.

'Through analysis and contemplation you will come to see that much of our misery, suffering, and pain really result from a self-centred attitude that cherishes one's own well-being at the expense of others. Much of the joy, happiness, and sense of security in our lives arise from thoughts and emotions that cherish the well-being of other sentient beings.

'In some sense the Bodhisattvas, the compassionate practitioners of the Buddhist path, are wisely selfish people, whereas people like ourselves are the foolishly selfish. We think of ourselves and disregard others, and the result is that we always remain unhappy and have a miserable time. The time has come to think more wisely, hasn't it? This is my belief.'[3]

Whenever I associate with others I will learn
To think of myself as the lowest among all
And respectfully hold others to be supreme
From the very depths of my heart.

In the words of the Dalai Lama:

'In the Buddhist tradition, compassion and loving kindness are seen as two sides of the same thing. Compassion is said to be the empathetic wish that aspires to see the object of compassion, the sentient being, free from suffering. Loving kindness is the aspiration that wishes happiness upon others. In this context, love and compassion should not be confused with love and compassion in the conventional sense. For example, we experience a sense of closeness towards people who are dear to us. We feel a sense of compassion and empathy for them. We also have strong love for these people, but often this love or compassion is grounded in self-referential considerations: "So-and-so is my friend", "my spouse", "my child", and so on. This kind of love or compassion is tinged with attachment because it involves self-referential considerations.

'Once there is attachment there is also the potential for anger and hatred to arise. Attachment goes hand in hand with anger and hatred. For example, if one's compassion towards someone is tinged with attachment, it can easily turn into its emotional opposite due to the slightest incident. Then instead of wishing that person to be happy, you might wish that person to be miserable.

'True compassion and love in the context of training of the mind is based on the simple recognition that others, just like myself, naturally aspire to be happy and to overcome suffering, and that others, just like myself, have the natural right to fulfil that basic aspiration.

'The essential feature of true compassion is that it is universal and not discriminatory. As such, training the mind in cultivating compassion in the Buddhist tradition first involves cultivating a thought of even-mindedness, or equanimity, towards all sentient beings. The practice of developing or cultivating equanimity involves a form of detachment. Sometimes when people hear about the Buddhist practice of detachment, they think that Buddhism is advocating indifference towards all things, but that is not the case. First, cultivating detachment, one could say, takes the sting out of discriminatory emotions towards others that are based on considerations of distance or closeness. You lay the groundwork on which you can cultivate genuine compassion extending to all other sentient beings.

'I think it is important to understand the expression "May I see myself lower than all others" in the right context. Certainly it is not saying that you should engage in thoughts that would lead to lower self-esteem, or that you should lose all sense of hope and feel dejected, thinking, "I'm the lowest of all. I have no capacity, I cannot do anything and have no power." This is not the kind of consideration of lowness that is being referred to here.

'The regarding of oneself as lower than others really has to be understood in relative terms. Generally speaking, human beings are superior to animals. We are equipped with the ability to judge between right and wrong and to think in terms of the future and so on. However, one could also argue that in other respects human beings are inferior to animals. Sometimes we engage in actions purely out of indulgence — we kill out of a sense of "sport", say, when we go hunting or fishing. So, in a sense, one could argue that human beings have proven to be inferior to animals. It is in such relativistic terms that we can regard ourselves as lower than others.

'Normally when we give in to ordinary emotions of anger, hatred, strong attachment and greed, we do so without any sense of restraint. Often we are totally oblivious to the impact our behaviour has on other sentient beings. But by deliberately cultivating the thought of regarding others as superior and worthy of your reverence, you provide yourself with a restraining factor. Then, when emotions arise, they will not be so powerful as to cause you to

Opposite: White Tara, associated with long life and healing

disregard the impact of your actions upon other sentient beings. It is on these grounds that recognition of others as superior to yourself is suggested.'[4]

> In all actions I will learn to search into my mind
> And as soon as an afflictive emotion arises,
> Endangering myself and others,
> Will firmly face and avert it.

The Dalai Lama explains the full significance of this verse:

'For a Buddhist practitioner, the real enemy is this enemy within — these mental and emotional defilements [which] give rise to pain and suffering. The real task of a Buddhadharma practitioner is to defeat this inner enemy. Since applying antidotes to these mental and emotional defilements lies at the heart of Dharma practice and is in some sense its foundation, the third verse suggests that it is very important to cultivate mindfulness right from the beginning.

'If you let negative emotions and thoughts arise inside you without any sense of restraint, without any mindfulness of their negativity, then in a sense you are giving them free rein. They can then develop to the point where there is simply no way to counter them. However, if you develop mindfulness of their negativity, then when they occur you will be able to stamp them out as soon as they arise. You will not give them the opportunity or the space to develop into full-blown negative emotional thoughts.

Opposite: Atisha (982–1054),
Indian teacher and author

'What is being suggested is the application of antidotes that are appropriate to specific negative emotions and thoughts. For example, to counter anger you should cultivate love and compassion. To counter strong attachment to an object you should cultivate thoughts about the impurity of that object, its undesirable nature and so on.

'To counter one's arrogance or pride, you need to reflect upon shortcomings in you that can give rise to a sense of humility. For example, you can think about all the things in the world about which you are completely ignorant. Take the sign language interpreter here in front of me. When I look at her and see the complex gestures with which she performs the translation, I haven't a clue what is going on, and to see that is quite a humbling experience.'[5]

I will learn to cherish beings of bad nature
And those pressed by strong sins and sufferings.
May I cherish them as the rarest find,
Like chancing upon a treasury of jewels.

When others feel jealous of me
And abuse and attack me wrongly,
I will learn to take all loss
And offer the victory to them.

When one whom I have benefitted with great hope
Unreasonably hurts me very badly,
I will learn to view that person
As an excellent spiritual guide.

In short, may I give to all, my mothers,
All help and happiness in this and future lives.
And may I respectfully take upon myself
All harm and suffering of my mothers.

I will learn to keep all these practices
Undefiled by the stains of the eight worldly conceptions,
And by understanding all phenomena as like illusions
Be released from the bondage of attachment.

When they first hear these verses, some people say: 'This is not for me. No way. My self-esteem is fragile enough as it is.'

That understandable first reaction may be a mistaken one, however, for several reasons. Firstly, the verses are not directives about how to behave, but how to think. They suggest a shift in motivation and perspective, in who and what are at the centre of our concerns. They challenge not a healthy sense of self but an exaggerated self-absorption, self-concern or self-ishness which excludes others and removes them to the fringes of our vision.

Secondly, these verses are an invitation to experiment with a different way of being in the world.

The point of trying out the *Eight Verses* in practice, especially when life is difficult for us, is to see what happens. What Buddhists say often happens is that the person who benefits is the practitioner. For example, when someone gets angry with us, we don't get upset in response. We retain a spaciousness that leaves room for alternatives, for new ways of dealing with the situation.

At times the benefits are immediate. For example, if someone provokes us, we start feeling tight, hot and tense, but then a Buddhist verse comes to mind: *I will offer victory to them.* That thought alone, even before we do anything, creates space and opens up options. It questions the seeming inevitability of bursting out with a habitual reaction. It short-circuits the knee-jerk reaction; we pause and allow a gap to open up into which new possibilities can emerge.

In practice these verses are like a lifeline. They show us that there are choices available in those moments when we need them.

We have plenty of buttons others can press. We have been trying to gain control, only to become someone quite pre-dictable — sometimes mean, sometimes worse. We are vulner-able and easily manipulated. It doesn't take much to bring out the worst in us. For some this takes the form of anger, for others it is seething resentment or jealousy, anxiety or depression.

From a Buddhist point of view, control isn't having everything fixed or tied down, because that is impossible. Control is a mind that is open to whatever arises, responding creatively, even in extreme situations.

The verses invite us not only to stop being available for manipulation but to develop new, positive qualities. They train the mind to be less conditioned, and work on basic qualities we need when things get tough.

One such quality is patience. We don't find patience as a subject on the school or university syllabus. Many parents don't know how to teach it to their children: some find it difficult to demonstrate by example. Yet there are times in even the most charmed life when things don't go the way we want, and there's not a lot that can be done about it except to be patient and wait for things to change. If we have been patient with situations that we can't change, we are open and relaxed when the opportunity for change does arise. If we are impatient, frustrated and uptight because things didn't happen as they were supposed to, we may not even notice that the moment of opportunity has come.

So who can teach us patience? Buddhists have observed over the centuries that the ideal teacher — someone who gives us little choice but to be patient — is someone who gets angry with us. If we can go with the situation and not take it too seriously, we will have learned something and created space both for ourselves and for the other person, whose anger might even subside because it is not met with aggression. This is not giving up or being a doormat. It's smart, skilful and 'spacious'.

The *Eight Verses* invite us to experience our emotions afresh, especially if they are memorised, and this is where it gets interesting. If someone starts yelling at us, whatever our initial reaction, with these verses we now have a new space in which to mindfully experience our habitual response.

We may notice that such situations trigger a cascade of habitual reactions. A classic pattern is when instead of just staying with a feeling of jealousy, for example, a whole internal dialogue opens and in a moment we have a complete routine going on in the mind. Something such as this: 'Why does this have to happen to me? I can't stand it. It's not fair. You are doing this to me. Stop it.'

This cascade happens so fast that it is subconscious. It takes a conscious effort to be mindful of the routine we put ourselves through. We can then observe that the outcome of the cascade is often a situation that becomes worse and worse, more solid, unworkable and impossible. We may even get angry about being angry or depressed about being depressed.

For example, by tasting the actual flavour of our jealousy, we experience ourselves anew. Instead of being totally bound up in acting out that jealousy, a part of us becomes available to just observe and not rush in with judgements and routines. The verses may at first seem to impose a new discipline, yet they are to be implemented gradually and not by force.

The point of the *Eight Verses* is to transform our mind. The self is no longer on centre stage to make us happier. This transformation is a way of lightening up and letting others in. It is a recognition that the mind is cluttered with much that ought to help but actually hinders. We let go of what doesn't work so that there is room to accommodate a fresh approach.

Perhaps we first approach Buddhism in the hope that it will offer us a technique, a way of overcoming a blind spot. But Buddhism offers much more than that. It is a basic shift of perspective, a way of seeing everything from a fresh angle, and it begins with transforming the mind. Ultimately, this leads to full awakening, or becoming a Buddha.

The final lines of the *Eight Verses* put it all in perspective:

By understanding all phenomena as illusions
Be released from the bondage of attachment.

To awaken is to discover that what we have taken so seriously is actually a construct, something that lacks substance and exists only as long as the causes and conditions that brought it into being persist. These verses show us how we have imprisoned ourselves unnecessarily by making our own emotions more solid than they need to be. We discover that we are addicted to things and situations, and to expectations that we think will cause happiness but which will actually lead to disappointment and frustration. We are addicted to our own suffering, and it takes a very direct message to turn our mind in a new direction.

To see phenomena as dreamlike, or as illusions, loosens the grip of these addictions. Our attachments to control, to managing phenomena and to having everything knowable and known are the addictions that enslave us and others. In the *Eight Verses* we pray that we may develop the ability to help all beings. May they too be freed from all bonds by the fundamental wisdom that knows all things to be illusory.

Atisha's *Lamp for the Path to Enlightenment*

Atisha's *Lamp for the Path to Enlightenment*[6] is poetry, literally and figuratively. In sixty-eight concise and exquisite verses, Atisha produced a miracle of miniaturisation, summing up the experience not only of the historic Buddha, but of a millennium and a half of Buddhist meditative awakening throughout India and beyond.

For a thousand years since, these verses have steadily shone their light on what we most need, but mostly miss: how to live a grounded, authentic life, in freedom from the phantoms that haunt us not only in our dreams but during our waking hours. Atisha's lamp illumines the dark corners of our lives with the clear light of understanding of the insubstantiality of every-thing to which we normally cling.

The entire heritage of Buddhism is present in Atisha's 274 short lines, from the initial steps towards immediate happi-ness to the most sublime insight into the freedom of emptiness, and on to the tantric direct methods.

It all begins with motivation. If personal happiness is the greatest goal we can imagine, meditation practice proceeds and there is a result. But Atisha makes it clear from the beginning that we could aim much higher. We could be mindful of the future, of the long-term consequences of how we live now and the choices we make (usually automatically and with little aware-ness). Atisha invites us to think not only of today's happiness, but of this life in its entire span, its inevitable transformation by death, and of future lives.

He then goes a step further, suggesting that we stand back a little from the preoccupations of the self, to better take in the view. To see expansively is to notice that we are not alone in seeking happiness. There's a world out there full of people and other beings with minds, all seeking the same goal. By stepping back from the insistent demands of the self, we create space in our minds and hearts for the struggles and desires of others.

From the outset Atisha asks us: what sort of person are you? Is the meaning of life for you just to get the most fun now? If so, you could be described as a person of limited capacity. Or are you aware of the longer-term consequences of your actions, but still basically thinking only of yourself? This describes a person of middling capacity. Or have you awoken to the reality that we all suffer dissatisfaction, we all want happiness and we are all confused about how to achieve it — and that there is a path of awakening? This describes a person of supreme capacity.

Atisha himself is totally dedicated to the path of supreme capacity, with its aspiration to gain ultimate enlightenment and thus have the capacity to be of real help to others, showing them a way through the confusions and anxieties of everyday life. He invites us to live up to our potential, and most of his poem contains the step-by-step process of how to do just that.

Atisha knows that we will need help. We would like to think of ourselves as heroic, but often it takes more than willpower to adopt consistent practice of the path to enlightenment. Atisha's lamp reveals methods to strengthen that initial resolve to work for all and for the long term.

He begins by making us active participants in the teachings rather than passive spectators. We are invited to take refuge, to join the family of practitioners, to find a new home among those who together take the path to discovering their supreme capacity. Atisha and the Dalai Lama invite us to enact the ritual of declaring to ourselves, and in company, that we take refuge in the Buddha, his teachings and the community of practitioners — Buddha, Dharma and Sangha.

To take refuge can be a turning point, but it is not salvation. It does not mean that from now on we have to be heroically altruistic and forget our own needs. It does not mean that we have to renounce whatever faith we believe in. It is an invitation to be wholesome and to discover there is much more to life than scratching the surface of the material world for creative happiness that usually proves elusive. In this sense, taking refuge is not only opening an inner door but also closes the outer door of self-obsession. It enables us to get on with what matters despite the fascination of endless distractions, knowing that life is short.

We could go overboard in our discovery of this new family we can belong to, and think we must ditch everything we have held dear. To take refuge doesn't mean giving up our possessions, our family or job. That would be a mistake, from a Buddhist point of view. It means that we no longer invest in them the power to make us everlastingly happy. We let go of the exaggerated expectations we have had that they can bring us what can only come from within. We let them be themselves, without attachment.

Taking refuge is a brief but formal ceremony, and to

take refuge directly from the Dalai Lama is a rare opportunity. Many Buddhists who have already taken refuge renew this vow in the presence of the Dalai Lama in order to refresh their commitment.

The Dalai Lama invites us to join him in a collective act of imagination. On a stage which is adorned with paintings and statues of Buddhas and representations of the enlightened mind; with flowers, bowls of offerings and incense; the Dalai Lama invites us to add our creative imagination. We are encouraged to multiply the Buddhas and offerings, to fill the mind and populate the stage before us with all the Buddhas and Bodhisattvas past, present, and future, who assemble to witness and rejoice in our vow to awaken. What matters is that we have a sense that we are not alone, that there are many who have taken this path before us and have awakened.

This is also a moment for letting go of unfinished business. We can now openly acknowledge and release the hold of regrets, guilt, shame, past hurts and resentments that haunt our minds. What's done cannot be undone, and if we relive the past we can't get on with life. We can learn from our mistakes, and then move on. We can let go.

Atisha's poem says that we should take this vow from a well-qualified spiritual teacher. This means, above all, someone who lives by that vow, whose every breath, word and deed is suffused with the intention to attain and communicate enlightenment; someone who, in Atisha's words, 'lives by the vow and has the confidence and compassion to bestow it'.

Verse 9

And with strong faith in the Three Jewels,
Kneeling with one knee on the ground
And your hands pressed together
First of all take refuge three times.

Verse 10

Next, beginning with an attitude
Of love for all living creatures,
Consider beings, excluding none,
Suffering in the three bad rebirths,
Suffering birth, death, and so forth.

Verse 11

Then, since you want to free these beings
From the suffering of pain,
From suffering and the causes of suffering
Arouse immutably the resolve
To attain enlightenment.

At the Dalai Lama's invitation we kneel, one knee on the floor, one at the chest, and we recite the refuge prayer three times:

I go to the Buddha for refuge,
I go to the Dharma for refuge,
I go to the Sangha for refuge.

The Dalai Lama explains:

'When we encounter some suffering, or when we encounter fright or fear, we naturally tend to look towards someone who has the capacity to protect us, to help us. And having found such a protector, such a refuge, then we wholeheartedly confide in that object of refuge, that object of protection. We decide mentally and dispose ourselves to that object of refuge. That is the meaning of taking refuge.

'All the major religious traditions of the world follow their own teacher, and trust and take refuge in their teacher. Likewise in Buddhism also we take refuge to Buddha Shakyamuni. In Buddhism the most important thing is the teaching of the Buddha. We do not say that the teaching of Buddha Shakyamuni is great because Buddha Shakyamuni is great. It is vice versa. Buddha Shakyamuni is great because the teaching that Buddha Shakyamuni has given is based on reason, logic, and it helps remove suffering. The more you study, practise and meditate on the teaching of the Buddha the more you find truth and benefit in it. Because of this then you can conclude that the teacher who taught this teaching is a great teacher, a valid teacher.'[7]

Having taken refuge, we start to see the path ahead. We want to free others from their confusions and afflictive emotions, and we know we need to change if we are to live up to that aspiration. But it's only natural that such a big picture comes and goes, and we often revert to the habit of thinking only of ourselves. We are learning new habits, and usually this feels awkward at first.

We needn't expect too much of ourselves. What matters is not whether our determination to awaken wavers, but that we renew it. Nothing renews our firm determination as much as bringing to mind the suffering of others. We can include in this our own sufferings and anxieties because we aren't doing this to the exclusion of the self. That would be extreme. Putting self into perspective doesn't mean denying ourselves and our needs. This is the middle way, not an either/or situation. We liberate ourselves through our commitment to liberate others.

The ending of old habits takes discipline, but it is not a punitive approach. It is a process of purification of bodily and verbal actions, and especially a purification of the mind that habitually thinks too much, strategises and calculates too much, in the mistaken belief that this is what life in the material world is all about.

To purify is also to simplify and let go. Rather than fighting ourselves, we accept ourselves as we are, by experiencing the actuality of what is. Acceptance makes it much easier to change what needs to be changed, and to restrain when restraint is appropriate.

Verse 27

From this moment onwards
Until I attain enlightenment,
I shall not harbour harmful thoughts,
Anger, avarice or envy.

Verse 28

I shall cultivate pure conduct,
Give up wrong doing and desire
And with joy in the vow of discipline
Train myself to follow the Buddhas.

Verse 29

I shall not be eager to reach
Enlightenment in the quickest way,
But shall stay behind till the very end,
For the sake of a single being.

We can all decide to do no harm. This is the beginning
of the active non-violence of which the Dalai Lama often
speaks. To do no harm is common sense and includes not
killing, lying or stealing; not getting so intoxicated that we
lose control; and not engaging in inappropriate sexual activity
where someone's feelings end up getting hurt. These are basic
Buddhist vows we can take.

Beyond doing no harm, we can actually do good. To genuinely do good is to be attuned to who and where others are, rather than assume we know what is best for them. It also means being mindful of our motives and expectations. If we do something for others and they aren't appreciative, or they don't act on our advice and we get upset, we are acting selfishly and conditionally.

Atisha shows us how to hack through the undergrowth of our habits, uprooting weeds and planting fragrant flowers in their place. This process seems endless, but we must begin somewhere. As long as habit constricts our view — so that all we see is whatever seems relevant to ourselves — we can't make progress.

Exactly halfway through his sixty-eight verses the graded path suddenly gets steeper, but the view from it is wonderfully spacious. The lamp Atisha holds up for us no longer illuminates just the next step but a great vista, as he introduces us to the Mahayana Buddhist perspective. He reveals to us the truth of emptiness as the nature of all that exists in the mind and in the world. Shunyata (emptiness) is the great engine of liberation. If we see that everything we crave or shun, everything we aspire to and avoid is without inherent existence, we are profoundly free. No longer are we limited to choosing between this and that, rooting out bad habits and cultivating good ones. We are now able to cut through the fundamental cause of all our dissatisfactions at once.

It's easy to say that nothing exists inherently. Theoretically it makes sense to assert that whenever we closely examine anything we take to be an independent, self-existing thing, its 'thing-ness' is not to be found. For example, there is no essential 'chairness' to be found in a chair, or in its parts. 'Chair' is just a label that, for the sake of convenience, we attach to a particular assemblage of parts, which has a certain functionality for as long as it lasts, before it inevitably falls apart. There's no disputing this, but how can such common sense set us free?

In fact, labels, names and concepts have great power over us. We forget that they are devices invented by human minds for convenience. Indeed, we make them into laws of the universe. We are unlikely to be oppressed by our implicit belief that somewhere in a chair is an essential 'chairness'. But when it comes to the powerful concepts we have of 'me' and 'you' — that's a different story.

'I' experience 'me' in a very intimate, subjective and utterly personal way, in a private reality. 'I' experience 'you' as existing out there, at a distance. 'Me' is subjective, 'you' are objective. The distance set up by this subconscious approach is always problematic. We may structure our lives around trying to close the gap, drawing people closer in an attempt to bridge the gulf. Or we might feel driven to maintain the separation, keeping others out of our personal space. Either way, it sets up our life as a constant juggling act, requiring many negotiations with others to maintain the right distance, not too close or too far. It's not relaxing. It needs constant effort.

We may be able to relax and become much more accepting of others, and the world in general, if we do the practices Atisha lists in the first half of his text. If we develop mindfulness of what we all have in common (seeking happiness and meeting disappointment) we do much to soften our hard edges. But still I seem to exist in a fundamentally different way from you. I am in here, you are out there.

Verse 35

Just as a bird with undeveloped
Wings cannot fly in the sky,
Those without the power of higher perception
Cannot work for the good of living beings.

Verse 37

Those who want swiftly to complete
The collections for full enlightenment
Will accomplish higher perception
Through effort, not through laziness.

Atisha invites us to a higher perception that reframes everything. Higher perception is not some sort of mystical cosmic consciousness beyond this world; it is actually quite earthly and grounded, but it is beyond words.

Atisha gives us several verses to guide us towards the understanding and attainment of emptiness. We see through the fictions of the self and its pretence of solidity and continuity. This could be a rude shock, but it is also liberating. There's nothing to hang onto, no territory to defend. However, this in itself could remain a concept. To let the truth of emptiness take hold requires a stable, calm mind and an ability to concentrate, so that we can hold the mind in balance without drifting off into extremes. All the practices we do as we learn new habits are in preparation for this higher perception.

Having established wholesome habits in our lives, and having awoken to the emptiness of self and other, we can now see far across the mountains. The light that Atisha shines is our light, and its luminosity spreads afar. At this point we are ready for Atisha's great leap.

So far, on the path, we have been introduced to ways to cultivate good habits of loving kindness and active compassion, enabling us to engage skilfully with others in real-life situations.

In the world of things and people, feelings, emotions and concepts, we are learning how to live constructively and wholesomely, motivated to awaken so we can assist those who remain confused. We are beginning to dissolve the distance between 'me' and 'you' by discovering that we all exist in the same way, which is empty and lacking in anything inherent. In other words, we are awakening to the ultimate truth of how everything exists, as a product of causes and conditions. When we discover that, we are beyond concepts. We can meditate without concepts. This is natural relaxation. Things are as they are, seemingly infinitely different, yet all existing in the same way.

Now is the moment at which all of these paths come together. Compassion and insight into emptiness are the two wings we need in order to fly. And Atisha uses this image, of a bird developing and unfolding its wings, then soaring. Once aloft, we see not only far, but forever. Our lamp illuminates all.

Atisha shows us that wisdom and skilful means must go together, or we remain enslaved and can do little for others. We come to grips with happiness in the material world, first through skilful new habits, then by cutting to the core of all problems. We can soar into the sky and go wherever we choose, including coming back to the nest where it all began. But this time we don't cling possessively and exclusively to the nest of 'me' and 'mine', which makes all the difference in the world.

The initiation ceremonies

During his visit to Australia in 2002, the Dalai Lama is bestowing at least two initiations — those of Chenrezig (*Avalokiteshvara* in Sanskrit) and Drol Kar (known in English as White Tara). Before introducing these particular deities, we'll examine what it means to participate in an initiation ceremony.

Tibetan Buddhism belongs to the Mahayana Buddhist tradition, which includes the practice of Vajrayana or Tantra. The tantric path is often regarded as a short-cut to enlightenment and is popular in modern societies where time is of the essence. However, the tantric path can be counterproductive, even risky, without proper grounding in the foundations of Buddhist study and practice. Most people study for some time with a qualified and experienced teacher before embarking on tantric practice, and the Dalai Lama, among other great Tibetan teachers, emphasises the necessity for tantric practitioners to have the close guidance of a qualified tantric master.

Initiations form an important part of tantric Buddhism and are usually offered to students after they have undertaken some serious study of Buddhist scriptures. However, they can also be offered as a blessing to the general public. In these instances, the *mantra* of the deity is given, but it is not necessary for those receiving the initiation to commit themselves to lifelong daily practice. It is considered that just receiving the blessing can be of lasting and valuable benefit.

The term 'initiation' is *wang* in Tibetan and *abhisheka* in Sanskrit, which can be translated as 'the meeting of the two minds', those of the teacher and the student. Sometimes it's also called an 'empowerment'. During this ceremony the teacher attempts to convey the 'power' of the truth of a particular teaching according to his or her understanding.

There are a number of Tibetan Buddhist centres in Australia and New Zealand where initiations are given by lamas. Initiations can only be given by someone properly qualified, who may be known as the 'guru', 'lama', 'teacher' or 'master'. During the initiation a connection is forged between the teacher, the deity and the person receiving the empowerment. The teacher bestows the empowerment for a particular Buddhist deity (known as a *yidam*) in order to transfer the qualities of the deity to the student. The deity is sometimes seen as a devotional being. The tantric teachings maintain that we all have a divine quality, and the purpose of taking an initiation is to manifest the qualities and aspects of the deity in our own behaviour.

The deity can be considered an archetype, representing an aspect of human potential, and as the enlightened mind to which we can aspire. The more we do deity practice, the more familiar we become with the pure thoughts and actions of the enlightened mind. This can help us to react to situations with more positive impulses in our daily lives, instead of reacting with habitual defensiveness, anger, fear or other emotional responses. For example, Chenrezig symbolises the essence of compassion; by habitually turning our minds to his quality of enlightened compassion we are training in the natural expression of it.

During the initiation we use our imagination to visualise the deity above the crown of our head or in front of us, or we may visualise ourselves as the deity. Many people find that they experience feelings of bliss or inspiration as the blessings of the deity enter and are absorbed into their heart. After receiving an initiation or empowerment, we can recall these feelings, keeping them fresh and active. When faced with difficult situations or any kind of distress, we can remember what the deity symbolises and feel the state of mind associated with it. To do this effectively we don't need to be Buddhist or belong to any religion.

We don't need to believe in gods or in reincarnation to understand how we can benefit from these practices. When our mind is agitated or we are stressed, we affect other people around us. Anything we can do to control our mind and defuse this agitation and stress can only be of benefit to ourselves and others. Deity practice achieves this.

The deities described on the following pages, Chenrezig and White Tara, are both associated with two essential Buddhist principles: wisdom, and active or enlightened compassion. By visualising these deities and reciting their mantras, we can develop these qualities in ourselves. This begins as an aspiration or a wish and as the practice continues and deepens we come closer to reaching our goal.

Each deity has a mantra which can be recited many times. Mantra is a Sanskrit term that literally means 'that which protects the mind'. This protection works at different levels. When our conscious mind is absorbed in reciting the mantra and visualising the deity it is temporarily freed or protected from its normal, endless chatter and confusion. At a deeper level, it is said that mantras are able to transform our inner being and are a link to less tangible states of consciousness. This is one reason that practitioners don't always feel the need to have a literal explanation of the mantra in order to recite it.

Chenrezig

Chenrezig is known as the Buddha or Bodhisattva of compassion. His Sanskrit name is Avalokiteshvara, which translates as 'the great compassionate one' or 'the teacher who looks on all beings, bestowing happiness on them'. In China he is known as the deity Kuan Yin.

The Dalai Lama is regarded by Tibetans and many

Buddhists as the living embodiment of Chenrezig. The Dalai Lama's unshakeable commitment to non-violence and compassion at every level and to every being is an example of Chenrezig's qualities. The Dalai Lama shows us how we can transform our mind and actions in this way. We can develop the capacity to respond to the most harrowing circumstances with love, acceptance and a non-violent attitude. The practice of love and compassion is the basis for a life of harmony.

Chenrezig is depicted in either a four- or thousand-armed form, and is white in colour. In the four-armed aspect he has one face and sits upon a lotus and moon disc. His two hands are pressed together at his heart, holding a wish-fulfilling jewel, symbolic of his compassionate intent. His right hand holds a crystal rosary, symbolising his wish to free all beings from suffering. In his left hand he holds a flower, symbolising his pure compassionate motivation.

In his thousand-armed aspect, Chenrezig has eleven faces and a thousand arms, and in the palm of each hand there is an eye. These eyes and hands symbolise the fact that he can see the suffering of all sentient beings and that he is willing and able to reach out to us all to alleviate our suffering.

According to legend, Chenrezig once took a vow to save all beings from the sufferings of samsara. But when he realised the enormity of his vow, his body exploded into myriad pieces.

Amitabha Buddha and the Bodhisattva Vajrapani reassembled the pieces into this more powerful form of Chenrezig, with eleven heads, a thousand arms and a thousand eyes, so that he could reach out to help more beings and gaze over them with greater vigilance. Vajrapani and Amitabha then added their own heads to crown Chenrezig's nine faces.

Mantra of Chenrezig

Om mani padme hum — pronounced 'om mani pay-may hum' (sometimes *hum* is pronounced 'hung'). Translated as 'the jewel in the lotus', the entire meaning of the Buddhist path is contained in these six syllables. *Om* refers to the body, speech and mind of the Buddhas, which is what we are hoping to achieve by developing our minds. *Mani* means jewel, and refers to all the method aspects of the path. *Padme* means lotus and refers to the wisdom aspect of the path. By uniting both method and wisdom we can purify our minds and completely develop our potential. *Hum* refers to the mind of all the Buddhas. The jewel is also compassion, the embodiment of Chenrezig. The lotus is a particularly classical Buddhist image, used as a metaphor for our capacity to transcend our ordinary way of being. The roots of the lotus are in the mud at the bottom of the pond yet the stem rises through the water to produce a pure and perfect flower, which sits just slightly above the surface of the pond and is completely unstained by the muddy water. This flower is a symbol of the compassionate, enlightened mind.

Tibetans use the Chenrezig mantra not only during prayer or practice sessions but also in daily life. It is readily on their lips whenever they see or hear of an object which arouses their compassion, such as a friend becoming ill or a small dead animal on the side of the road. Reciting it at such times not only reminds the practitioner to feel compassion but also is intended to bring the compassion of Chenrezig straight to the suffering being.

White Tara

The name Tara translates as 'she who liberates', and White Tara is an aspect of this deity so greatly loved by Tibetans. She is the female principle, the protector and saviour, one to whom they turn in times of danger, distress, risk or fear. She is the female Bodhisattva of mercy and compassion. Just as Chenrezig is sometimes described as the 'patron deity' of Tibet, Tara is his counterpart — the 'patron goddess' of Tibet.

In her green and white form Tara is believed to have manifested from two tears which fell from Chenrezig's eyes, when he looked around the different realms of existence and witnessed such intense and widespread suffering. In her white form, Tara is especially invoked for the pacifying rituals of longevity, healing and altruistic activity. In times of ill-health, or life-threatening danger, it is useful to visualise White Tara and recite her mantra, either for ourselves or on behalf of another person.

White Tara is always depicted sitting cross-legged on a lotus and moon disc. Her right hand is in the wish-granting *mudra* (gesture) of providing beings with their desires. Her left hand is placed at her heart, granting refuge, with the thumb and forefinger pressed together to symbolise the unity of the method and wisdom practices. The three other fingers of that hand are raised to symbolise the Three Jewels of Refuge — the Buddha, the Dharma and the Sangha.

In each of her palms and soles is an eye, symbolising the five method perfections of generosity, morality, patience, effort and concentration (represented by her five fingers and toes) that depend upon the sixth perfection, the development of wisdom. These four eyes symbolise her boundless compassion, the 'four immeasurables' of compassion, love, sympathetic joy and equanimity. The three eyes on her face symbolise the perfection of her body, speech and mind — the purity of her conduct, words and thoughts. Above her head is Amitabha Buddha, whose name means 'infinite light' and who represents the limitless and luminous aspect of our nature.

Mantra of White Tara

Om tare tuttare ture mama ayur punye pushtim kuri ye soha — the mantra of White Tara translates as, 'I prostrate to the Liberator, the Mother of all the Victorious Ones.'

Becoming familiar with these deities helps us to get in touch with our own finer qualities, and to gradually come to believe that we are capable of such great goodness as Chenrezig and Tara represent. Their love, friendliness, compassion and protectiveness can be our friends too.

In difficult times we can call out to deities such as Chenrezig and Tara for help. Like all the Buddhas, as soon as they hear our cry for help, they respond. We may experience an almost immediate calming of the mind and may feel comforted, or we may realise later that something has shifted, ever so slightly.

We use our creative imagination in these practices, and when we stop to think about it, we realise that our whole world is actually created by our mind. If we activate our connection with these embodiments of protective compassion when we need protection, we create the right conditions for help to be available to us. We need to do all we can to live wisely, safely and compassionately, by taking full responsibility for our lives, but when we invoke the power of the compassion of all the Buddhas, it is not just for ourselves but for all sentient beings. This is the practice of manifesting compassion in our world.

The procession for the
Dalai Lama's arrival
(**above**) and the Dalai
Lama giving a teaching
(**left**), Quang Minh
Temple, Melbourne,
1996.

Above: The Dalai Lama bestowing blessings, Sydney Harbour, 1996.
Left: The Dalai Lama and Sangha in Australia, 1996.
Below: Geshe Sonam Thargye.

CHAPTER FIVE

A LAMP FOR THOSE WHO SEEK LIGHT:
Buddhism in Australia and New Zealand

Buddhism in Australia

In the late 1920s Marie Beuzeville Byles, a young woman from Sydney, regularly joined her friends bushwalking in the forests around Sydney. Today bushwalking is popular; then it was revolutionary, especially as a recreation for women. Marie Byles, with companions Paddy Pallin and Myles Dunphy, were pioneers of the idea that the Australian bush was beautiful and invigorating rather than something to be cleared or avoided because it was dangerous, monotonous, strangely silent and not very European.

Marie Byles, a no-nonsense Sydney lawyer with strong feminist sympathies, strode through the Australian bush and sought mountains to climb. She was drawn not only to the worn and ancient Australian mountains but the more challenging peaks of China and Burma drew her upward also. She was a 'material girl'. Spirituality, she said, was among those 'things for which, as a university student in the early 'twenties, I had a supreme contempt. If others suggested people might be swayed by loving kindness, we dismissed the idea as Victorian nonsense and turned away to hide our embarrassed blushes. People were governed by the laws of supply and demand, purchasing power parity and that sort of thing.'[1]

Hers was a fulfilling life, with a busy law practice balanced by the quiet of the bush. 'For those who like peace and solitude,' she wrote in the 1960s, 'Sydney is wonderfully situated, for it is surrounded by barren sandstone country unattractive to the farmer, so that within fifteen miles of what is spoken of as "the second city of the Empire", there are wild bushlands, or forested hills.'[2]

An inner voice beckoned Marie Byles, however, and she listened to it. On her adventures climbing Burmese peaks before World War II, she passed many Buddhist monasteries whose stillness and peace increasingly drew her to investigate further.

After the war she was able to return to Asia, but was no longer able to climb mountains, as foot surgery had left her in chronic pain. This encounter with the truth of suffering sent her inside the monasteries on what she describes as her 'path to inner calm'. There she learned to meditate deeply and to realise the Four Noble Truths taught by the Buddha as her own experience. For Marie Byles, the rebel, it was not a straight-forward surrender to the teachings. The idea of bowing to a monk was not easy for her to accept:

'This was wholly opposed to my, not merely protestant, but Unitarian-dissenting background, and still more to an innate Quakerism which insists that there is no such thing as a professional priest, and that only in so far as the individual can let the Inner Light of the Spirit shine through, can he be regarded as a spiritual teacher or leader.'[3]

Marie Byles, who bowed to no one, did bow to the Buddha and his teachings. She discovered basic realities which transcended gender, class, race and other differences. After Buddhism had become part of each moment for her and a new way of experiencing things, she returned to Sydney. After many years of pain she experienced 'the restoration of perfect health, due, so far as could be seen, simply to accepting the body's pain and the office worries without resentment or ill-will.'[4]

In the 1960s she wrote several books about her adventures including her discovery of Buddhism, and a tenderly devotional biography of the Buddha. She made sure women featured in the story, women of 'vivid personality with decided opinions and forceful character', rather like herself.

Hers is the story of one of Australia's Buddhist pioneers.

The history of Buddhism in Australia stretches back over 150 years to the gold rushes which brought Chinese miners seeking their fortunes over the seas to the New Gold Mountain — as they called Australia. Since then, Buddhism has touched the lives of many Australians and New Zealanders and has come to mean much more than personal calm and inner peace. Over the generations, the number of Buddhist practitioners in these countries has increased as has the availability of teachers with full-lineage credentials.

Buddhism has come to resonate with a range of lifestyle choices. More and more people have discovered practical uses for Buddhism in their lives. Painters, poets, dancers, actors and writers have been especially drawn to the Buddhist centres now flourishing in Australian and New Zealand cities and towns. What draws them is perhaps the possibilities and expressiveness that Buddhism seems to unlock. Nurses, doctors and therapists join Buddhist communities to learn how to give to others without burning out. Lawyers, executives and other professionals say they find in Buddhist practice a clarity and precision, together with a relaxation and flexibility, which combine to promote decisive and inclusive leadership.

Practitioners consistently report that meditation shifts

their perspective, opens up the bigger picture and tames the mind. Meditation can reframe life, enabling practitioners to feel less stressed by the pressures and demands of a career, and to find more workable ways of meeting the needs of others without sacrificing their own needs. Meditation reminds us that we need not feel victimised by circumstances, that even in extreme situations there is always a choice of response. In today's world, such suppleness of mind is invaluable.

As Buddhist practice broadens and deepens, it changes — what once was a highly individualistic practice becomes more of a mutually supportive process in communities. What was strongly intellectual and philosophical is now softened by the awakening of trust in the path, and in communities of practitioners past and present. There is now a greater devotion to teachers or those who show the way. Recent census figures reveal that the majority of Australian Buddhists are female, and this is increasingly true of instructors and teachers too.

Australia and New Zealand have become two of the best places on earth for experiencing the full diversity of Buddhist approaches suited to the diversity of human personalities. Multicultural societies have been open to migration by people from the whole spectrum of Asian societies, deeply touched over centuries by Buddhism. In each country Buddhism took on the cultural forms of the host society rather than declare the earlier established faiths heretical. When we walk into a Thai temple, for example, it looks quite different from a Japanese Zen or Tibetan Buddhist temple. There is a remarkable diversity in imagery, aesthetics and outward display.

In Australia and New Zealand, Buddhists from all over Asia can have meaningful encounters. Historically, Buddhists from Sri Lanka would have had almost no opportunity to meet Buddhists from Mongolia; nor would those from Cambodia have connected with those from Tibet. But in Australian cities, especially in Sydney and Melbourne, a Vietnamese temple may be only a street or a suburb away from a Tibetan meditation centre, and there are many opportunities for communities to meet.

Differences remain, but the monks, nuns and teachers at the temples say they are finding a shared experience of insight into reality that transforms lives. One temple may offer traditional devotions and opportunities for lay people to build merit by making offerings; while another temple nearby may seem more austere — emphasising logic, analysis and close attention to the momentary sensations of the body. What do these various communities have in common? The teachers say they all encourage people to experience fully the fundamental truth that nothing in the material world can be trusted to last and nothing external provides true refuge, but that the human mind can be entirely happy and free from dissatisfaction.

This diversity of Buddhism is its strength. Diversity encourages people to seek until they find a teacher or a community that resonates with them. But once they embark on the path, all roads seem to lead to a deepening insight into universal truths of the human condition rather than the specifics of a particular culture. And the diversity will endure. In Australia and New Zealand today, there is no sense that only one style of practising is correct.

A list of Buddhist communities in Australasia is included at the end of this book. This brief survey of Buddhism in Australia and New Zealand concentrates on the Tibetan Buddhist communities.

August 30, 2002 is the fiftieth anniversary of the arrival of the first professional Buddhist teacher in Australia, an elderly American nun named Venerable Dhammadina who was ordained in Shanghai in the 1920s. She arrived in Melbourne, where she told the press that she intended setting up an institute for the 'science of Buddhism'. Her story is remarkable. She introduced Australians to Chenrezig (Avalokiteshvara), the incarnation of compassion, to whom she was greatly devoted, and taught for a year, mostly in Sydney. Following her visit, the Buddhist Society of New South Wales was formed in 1953, and a year later the Buddhist Society of Victoria was established in Melbourne.

Early meetings of the Buddhist Society were leisurely and held in city cafes, coffee shops and bookshops. Amid the endless choice offered to us today, it's a jolt to discover that only fifty years earlier, even in the biggest cities, access to all manner of things Asian was confined to a couple of bohemian bookshops. Writer Peter Kelly was a young man then, he recalled:

'The bookshop became one of the few venues in Melbourne where one could find texts on Vedanta, Taoism, Buddhism, comparative religion and philosophy, yoga or art books on Chinese and Japanese painting. I recall the genteel atmosphere: polished floors, rugs and vases of flowers as well as chintzy armchairs for patrons to peruse books ... During meetings people squatted on the floor or perched on the counter; there were very few stools. The door was usually locked for meetings to prevent the intrusion of the general public. One participant recalls the meetings as somewhat secret and clandestine.'[5]

Monks from Sri Lanka and Burma began to visit Sydney and Melbourne regularly, but few stayed for long. A sense of community and of contemplative space grew when Elizabeth Bell placed her inner city Carlton home at the disposal of the Buddhist Society in 1968. (Thirty years later Elizabeth was awarded the Order of Australia for services to Buddhism in Australia.)

These early practitioners were divided over which aspects of Buddhism mattered. Some favoured a devotional approach, others wanted to steer clear of the traditions and ceremonies that had become a part of Buddhism in Eastern countries and concentrate on its psychology. And to some, 'an emphasis on meditation would have been welcome.'[6]

In 1972 a Sri Lankan monk, Somaloka, came to Australia and established Australia's first Buddhist temple since the gold rushes more than a century earlier. It opened in 1974 in the Blue Mountains, and Somaloka stayed on as spiritual director. A year later Wat Buddha-rangsee was established in Sydney, a gift to Australia by the Crown Prince of Thailand who had studied in Australia. He sent an English monk, Phra Khantipalo, to set up the temple and teach. Phra Khantipalo (now known simply as Lawrence Mills) has taught Australians for almost thirty years, and now runs a relaxed Tibetan Dzogchen community in tropical Cairns.

Theravadan centres and temples developed around the country, with resident Sangha (communities of practitioners) and teachers. Followers of the Mahayana traditions of China and Japan arrived in the 1950s and 1960s, and in 1961 the Soto Zen Buddhist Society was formed. Through the 1970s Zen groups were established in other states, and the Sydney Zen Centre opened in 1976.

After the Vietnam War ended in 1975, large numbers of refugees arrived in Australia by boat from Indo-China. Australia opened its doors, and many temples and schools were founded in major cities. The majority of Buddhist temples in Australia are from these South-East Asian traditions.

Some Buddhist centres are not affiliated with any one tradition. These include the Friends of the Western Buddhist Order, which has its roots in both Theravadan and Tibetan Buddhism, and the many Buddhist Societies in universities. New South Wales, Queensland and Victoria have Buddhist Councils to promote co-operation among Buddhist communities and inter-faith dialogue and they maintain lists of all centres.

The Tibetan Buddhist communities began in the late 1960s and early '70s, when Australians and New Zealanders started travelling to India and Nepal, where they met Tibetan lamas who were refugees. Many of these travellers stayed on to study Tibetan Buddhism, mainly in the North Indian Himalayan hill-station of Dharamsala, and in Kathmandu, Nepal.

Tibetan monks Lama Yeshe and Lama Zopa Rinpoche established a monastery outside Kathmandu and began teaching Westerners in a month-long intensive course in 1971. These courses are still offered today. In 1972 several Australians found their way to Kopan. Dr Nicholas Ribush and Marie Obst, now Yeshe Khadro, were the first Australians to be ordained in the Tibetan Buddhist tradition. They were responsible for introducing many of their friends to Buddhism and organising the visits of the lamas and the establishment of the early centres in Australia.

On returning to their own countries, the students were enthusiastic to continue their study and invited the lamas to visit. Lama Yeshe and Lama Zopa Rinpoche were the first Tibetan lamas to come to Australia. They arrived in 1974. Lama Yeshe taught in English, at a time when few Tibetans spoke English and fewer Australians knew a word of Tibetan. From the outset he taught Buddhist psychology. He tackled the '70s generation head on, saying to an Auckland audience in 1975:

'I've encountered a certain arrogance in the West, where some scientific materialists proudly proclaim, "I'm not a believer." They're so proud of their professed lack of belief in anything. But no matter who you think you are, you still need to know the characteristic nature of your own mind. If you don't, then no matter how much you talk about the shortcomings of attachment, you have no idea what attachment actually is or how to control it.

'When you study Buddhism, you are studying yourself, the nature of your own mind. Buddhism focuses on practical matters, such as how to lead your life, how to integrate your mind and how to keep your everyday mind peaceful and healthy.'[7]

On the Sunshine Coast in Queensland the lamas gave a month-long meditation course to two hundred students. The result was the first Tibetan Buddhist centre, the Chenrezig Institute, set amid pineapple plantations as local students offered much of their land to the lamas. Other centres soon followed.

Lama Yeshe formed the Foundation for the Preservation of the Mahayana Tradition (FPMT) and centres were opened in most Australian states and throughout New Zealand. The largest are the Chenrezig Institute in Queensland and the Tara Institute in Melbourne. There are now over twenty FPMT centres in Australia and New Zealand, some of which are residential. Six FPMT centres have resident geshes or lamas, who also teach in other centres. All centres provide regular teachings on meditation, Buddhist philosophy and psychology for beginners up to advanced level. Some also teach Tibetan language, yoga, art classes, children's classes and healing courses. Several retreats and intensive courses are held throughout the year, and lamas from overseas regularly tour the centres.

Geshe Tashi Tsering, based at the Chenrezig Institute, conducts a Buddhist Masters study programme, which is an intensive course running over several years. In Melbourne, Geshe Doga conducts weekend courses and an annual Easter retreat. He runs a study programme, in which about one hundred students are enrolled and tested regularly to assess how well they understand the teachings. For more intensive meditation practice FPMT has retreat centres, including one on Kangaroo Island in South Australia.

Some FPMT meditators take monastic vows. A monastery of rammed-earth adobe buildings for Western monks has been built in the whipstick mallee country at the Atisha Centre near Bendigo, Victoria, close to the gold fields where Buddhism first appeared in Australia, and there is a well-established community of about twenty Western nuns at the Chenrezig Institute in Queensland. Another FPMT project is the replication of Tibet's most beautiful and complex Gyantse stupa, now under construction at Bendigo and due for completion by 2010.

In Brisbane, a Buddhist hospice provides sensitive and

humane services for the terminally ill of any faith, and their relatives. Karuna Hospice was started by monk Pende Hawter in 1990. It has full-time, professional staff and provides round-the-clock assistance to help people in their own homes. Services include specialist palliative care nursing, family counselling and bereavement support, respite-care volunteer courses, spiritual and medical care. Other Buddhist hospices are Cittamani in the Sunshine Coast hinterland and the Hospice of Mother Tara in Bunbury, Western Australia. Another project has been the production of a best selling CD, featuring artists such as Madonna and the Beastie Boys. All profits go to the Dalai Lama's welfare fund for Tibetan refugees, and so far over $250,000 has been raised.

The Lama Yeshe Wisdom Archive digitises works of the founding lamas as well as selected teachings of the Dalai Lama and other Tibetan teachers, producing booklets for free distribution. Mandala Books is a not-for-profit distributor of Buddhist books, representing six overseas publishers and supplying books wholesale to bookshops, libraries and universities, and retail by mail order.

The Tibetan Buddhist Society has another series of Buddhist centres which are Gelugpa lineage organisations. They were established by Geshe Thubten Loden, who first came to Australia in 1976 at the invitation of Lama Yeshe. Geshe Loden was initially the resident teacher at the Chenrezig Institute, and formed the Tibetan Buddhist Society two years later. The Society is based just to the north of Melbourne, and has recently constructed a large traditional prayer hall. This centre opens its beautiful buildings and ten acres of gardens to the public each year, and is the venue for two Buddhist festivals annually which attract thousands of people. This chain has centres in Brisbane, Sydney and Perth as well as Melbourne.

Geshe Loden was born in 1924 in Tibet. Like all geshes, he undertook a rigorously intensive education involving memorisation, internalisation and the ability to spontaneously teach a large number of texts and meditational practices. He was put to the test in a lengthy examination in the presence of the Dalai Lama, where he was closely questioned by his examiners for hours at a time. He then toured the greatest monasteries for a further two-week examination, with the entire monastic assembly firing questions non-stop for twenty-four hours. Geshe Loden came equal first in this process.

Khejok Tulku Rinpoche was born in the 1930s in eastern Tibet and enrolled at the great Sera monastery in Lhasa, where he received his Geshe degree. He began to teach in Australia in 1986, and established the headquarters of his Institute of Buddhist Learning and Practice (IBLP) in Sydney in 1989. Since then, many more branches have been set up throughout Australia, Canada and Asia. He is also a qualified Tibetan medical practitioner and is known for his extensive knowledge of statue making, and astrological divination.

Other lamas with an Australian focus include Zasep Tulku, who is now based in Canada. Zasep Tulku first came to Australia in 1976 as the translator for Geshe Loden and gradually attracted a group of students. Illusion Farm, his centre in Tasmania, was established in the 1980s and had its own touring theatre troupe! Zasep Tulku continues to visit the rural centres of his community in several parts of Australia.

In September 1999, during a visit to India, Geshe Sonam Thargye issued a personal invitation to the Dalai Lama to visit Australia, and by doing so set in motion the Dalai Lama's visit to Australia and New Zealand in 2002. 'Through my own good fortune I had the opportunity to make this personal request and for the benefit of all Australians I am so deeply happy for everyone that His Holiness kindly agreed to come,' says Geshe Sonam.

Geshe Sonam Thargye is the resident teacher and spiritual director at the Drol Kar Buddhist Centre in Geelong, Victoria, which he established in 1999. Born in Tibet, he has been a monk since the age of seven, gaining his Geshe Lharampa degree in India in 1994. He returned to Tibet briefly to teach, before coming to Australia and settling in Geelong.

Traleg Kyabgon Rinpoche came to Australia in 1980, establishing the Kagyu Evam Buddhist Institute (KEBI) in Melbourne in 1982. From his inner Melbourne base, Traleg Rinpoche has provided a welcome for over a hundred visiting teachers of all Buddhist traditions as well as therapists, philosophers, theologians and healers at an annual Buddhist Summer School at his inner-city campus and at a forest retreat which also hosts a Buddhism and Psychotherapy conference every eighteen months. His Maitripa Contemplative Centre, past the vineyards of the Yarra Valley, in the foothills of the Great Dividing Range, sees a group of meditators spend three months in intensive practice each winter under the supervision of a retreat master. Each three-month session counts towards the traditional three-year retreat which Tibetans take as the classic qualification to become a lama. Few Australians have yet completed this.

This high lama of the Kagyu lineage encourages a balanced approach in which equal emphasis is placed on developing a comprehensive yet deep understanding of the teachings (view), steady meditation practice to actualise the teachings (meditation), and integration of meditative insight into daily life (action). His community presents a great range of Buddhist perspectives in its quarterly magazine, *Ordinary Mind*.

Sogyal Rinpoche, known world wide for his teachings on death and dying, has his Rigpa centres in all Australian capital cities, as well as in Newcastle, Broome, Alice Springs and other towns. Many people know that Buddhists have an especially clear understanding of death, and an appreciation of how to live life. This draws large numbers to Sogyal Rinpoche's teachings on his annual visits. He oversees a curriculum of progressive study and practice offered to Rigpa students around the world.

Sogyal Rinpoche's students have also established a 'bush telegraph' service for Australians and New Zealanders who live far from a Rigpa centre, consisting of a library system and a study circuit. In the latter, a series of study packs are regularly despatched through the post from student to student, containing written, audio and video teaching materials in line with the Rigpa curriculum.

At the instigation of Dilgo Khentse Rinpoche (one of the twentieth century's outstanding lamas and a teacher of the Dalai Lama), Dzongsar Khyentse Rinpoche established a retreat centre called Vajradhara Gonpa in 1986 in the Border Range bushland of northern New South Wales. This teacher of the royal family of Bhutan (and director of the 2000 film, *The Cup*), later founded a centre in Sydney in 1989. Named Siddhartha's Intent, its objectives are to 'develop world peace through action and education and to preserve and advance Buddhist teachings and traditions'.

Another charismatic lama is Chogyal Namkhai Norbu Rinpoche, who visits Australia regularly and has several Dzogchen communities throughout Australia, New Zealand and South-East Asia. On the flank of Mt Dromedary near Tilba in southern New South Wales, his students gather from afar for rural retreats which include meditative dance and yantra yoga. Committed students can choose to undertake a rigorous study programme overseen by Namkhai Norbu Rinpoche, in which their understanding, both theoretical and experiential, is assessed at each level.

Also in the Nyingma tradition is the Odiyana Buddhist Centre in Melbourne, whose founder, Lama David Christensen, has completed a four-year meditation retreat and practised under many great lamas. Odiyana holds regular meditation practice sessions and study courses, and also hosts Buddhist art exhibitions and performances. David Christensen is establishing a country retreat centre near Wilson's Promontory, one of Victoria's most spectacular stretches of coastline.

His Holiness Sakya Trizin, head of the Sakya school of Tibetan Buddhism, came to Australia in 1988, and established Sakya Tharpa Ling in Sydney in 1987. After the death of its resident lama, Gyalsay Tulku Rinpoche, in 1993 Sakya Trizin sent the young scholar Loppon Ngawang Dhamchoe to lead practices, give teachings and conduct retreats.

After teaching in New Zealand for several years, Lama Choedak Yuthok established Sakya Losal Choe Dzong in Canberra in 1987, and the Jamchen Buddhist Centre in Melbourne. Two major retreats are held each year: a White Tara retreat and a Calm Abiding retreat. Lama Choedak has established a study programme in Canberra which encompasses five years of study, research, writing, translating, contemplation, retreats, daily meditation practice, community service, discipline, morality and maintaining vows. This Buddhist teacher training programme has been undertaken by several students to date. Another Sakya centre, Sakya Choekhor Lhunpo, was established in Melbourne in 1997.

The Tibetan Gyuto monks have travelled Australia extensively since 1994. They offer the Australian public the chance to experience first-hand the ancient and unique practices that the Gyuto monks have been engaged in since their tradition was first established in 1475. Their public programmes extend to art galleries, museums, shopping centres, theatres, schools, universities and the bush.

The monks have chanted for world peace on the shores of Lake Eyre at dawn, on snow-covered mountains at Falls Creek, in the Daintree rainforest, out on the Great Barrier Reef, and in the desert at Maralinga. They have chanted in the Sydney Opera House and at the National Gallery of Victoria, as well as in many small communities such as Ceduna in South Australia, Geraldton in Western Australia, Tilba in New South Wales, and Kuranda in far North Queensland.

They conduct guided meditation sessions and retreats for the general public, offer stress-management workshops for health professionals and healing chants for the sick, and run classes in everything from Tibetan-style chanting to cooking. They are immensely popular wherever they go and have done an enormous amount to raise the profile of Tibetan Buddhism across the continent.

Although not all the Tibetan Buddhist communities have been included here, the teachers and centres mentioned convey something of the variety of traditions in Australia.

In the last few years a number of Buddhist projects have been founded, most of which focus on welfare and assistance to the general public. Many Buddhist centres are active in their local community, working with the sick and dying, with the drug addicted, with prisoners or with people recently released from prison. Other organisations run food kitchens and other assistance projects for the disadvantaged, often working alongside local charitable groups.

Many Buddhists are activists in political or green issues,

both locally and internationally. A number of students have returned to Buddhist countries where they work to help the local population or fundraise for welfare projects from Australia.

The charisma and calibre of their teachers is what makes these Buddhist communities viable. Australia and New Zealand are fortunate in having authentic teachers resident on a long-term basis, all of whom have the classical qualifications. Australia's Buddhist teachers encourage people to check the credentials of teachers carefully. It is helpful to know that over many centuries Buddhists have developed codes of practice and explicit rules of conduct.

Because Buddhism is not actually an *-ism* at all, in the sense of being 'a package of beliefs beyond verification', Buddhist teachers emphasise that nothing be taken on blind faith. Nothing is so, just because someone in authority says it is so. As Buddhism is not a set of beliefs, truly qualified teachers are those who have realised the teachings in their daily life and conduct and have tamed the mind.

Very seldom does a teacher attain such transformative awakening alone, without the close relationship of student and teacher. A long chain of teacher–student connections — a lineage traceable all the way back to the historic Buddha — is one of the qualifications of a trustworthy Buddhist teacher. Among Buddhist teachers, and at the start of a formal teaching, the first thing to be mentioned is this lineage of teachers stretching back over generations. The wars, revolutions, invasions and disasters of the twentieth century in Asia have made continuity of lineage difficult, but it is still the highest priority.

Those who suddenly or gradually feel a sense of connection with a teacher and a community of students, and who persevere with their meditation begin to experience a basic shift in their motivation. Instead of meditating for personal short-term benefit, a more expansive and inclusive perspective dawns as the sense of distance between self and other starts to dissolve. Mindfulness of the needs of not only this generation but of future generations grows, and an awareness of the consequences of action develops, leading to a more confident, spontaneous compassion towards all living beings.

The initiations and teachings the Dalai Lama has chosen for Australian and New Zealand audiences are directly geared towards encouraging this shift in motivation. Perhaps the Dalai Lama has chosen them because they fit the needs of the times. His first visit to Australia was in 1982, followed by tours in 1992 and 1996.

The Buddhist teachers of Australasia encourage practitioners to go deeper, develop greater fortitude and confidence,

and undertake longer retreats. Some teachers maintain the classic distinction held in most Buddhist cultures between ordained monastic practitioners and lay practitioners. If there is sufficient community support, this enables some people to take the monastic vows and wear the robes, dedicating their lives to practice. But not all teachers make a distinction between professional and lay practice.

In Asia, many people believe that monks and nuns serve the whole community by meditating, and thus they support their monasteries. But, often in Australia and New Zealand, Buddhist practice is seen as a purely personal quest and does not attract community support, so there is little basis for monasticism. Also in Asian countries there can be a considerable difference in status between the monks and the lay population. The responsibility of lay men and women is seen as developing merit for themselves by making offerings to the monks and nuns, rather than making meditative awareness a part of their own daily life. Teachers who do not ordain students encourage them to take on many aspects of monastic dedication to practice.

Marie Byles would have been particularly struck by the connections between Buddhists and the Maori, Aboriginal and Islander revivals. Had she lived to see the new attitudes to sacred land, respect for Indigenous land rights and land use, she would have been delighted. Buddhist practice has sensitised many to respect the oldest traditions and communities in New Zealand and Australia, and a number of Buddhists are actively engaged in work within Indigenous communities.

Sonam Rigzin is a Tibetan–Australian and former monk. He works in Aboriginal communities as translator for the Tibetan Gyuto monks. His experience in the outback may be a clue to the future of Buddhism in Australia:

'We spent months in the outback with Aboriginal people, working with them. The abbot of the Gyuto monks talked with some of the elders of the Pitjantjatjara. Our abbot is a powerful presence, you can feel it. Aboriginal elders sense in him a man, like themselves, who has experienced much and learned much.

'When Tibetans and Aborigines meet, it's a meeting of equals. It doesn't start with any of the tensions you get between black and white. We don't have a formula, we don't teach Buddhism, we don't use jargon, we just manifest what it is about being human that we all have in common. Above all, we don't preach. We don't tell people how things are or what they should do. If no one comes when we arrive in a remote community, that's fine, we just do our thing, start our chanting and people drift in; after it's been going for an hour or two, people really get into it.

'The monks are from a tantric college. Tantra means working with whatever energy is in the air, taking whatever is, rather than striving to construct what ought to be. We touch the compassion in everyone, which is nothing magical because our starting point, not just as a belief but as our experience, is that all beings naturally have compassion. If you observe insects you can see that even they display compassion.

'People often muddle sympathy with compassion. Compassion arises naturally, and it is active. Sympathy is invoked; it's a conscious decision to feel sympathy. Compassion is confidence, self-confidence that I can act; I can do something to fix a situation. The root of suffering is self-hatred. This is simple logic, nothing to do with East or West. When you don't like yourself, you hurt others, and action taken in that state only hurts you more.

'The Aborigines still have their land, which is everything to them. When they discovered we had lost our land they took our posters and started sticking them on every desert bush. They were all fired up; they said they wanted to march on Canberra. Often we show people how to dissolve their anger. We talk about how we lost our land, and they can see that even though we lost everything, we are happy. We don't forget or ignore that loss; in fact we always mobilise people's energies for the Tibetan cause. But we are also showing, by example, by the shared experience of being together, that anger is not the only response to dispossession.

'We are a reminder, a pointer to the goodness in everyone. Our attitude is that you begin by looking after yourself, feeling good about yourself, then that's one less person for others to worry about.'[8]

Buddhism in New Zealand

Before 1970 there is little on record of the history of Buddhism in New Zealand. There were certainly practitioners among Chinese immigrants during the early years of the gold rush in the nineteenth century. In the mid-twentieth century Sir Edmund Hillary made his famous ascent of Mt Everest and started a long-term relationship with the Sherpa people of Nepal which continues to prosper, but New Zealanders were very unaware of the Buddhist way of life until the 1970s.

In the winter of 1973, Namgyal Rinpoche visited New Zealand with about eighty-five of his students, mostly from

Canada. They rented summer cottages around the shore of Lake Rotoiti near Rotorua (North Island) and held a three-month meditation retreat. Nearly thirty of these people liked New Zealand so much they decided to stay. In 1974 the Sphere Group of New Zealand was founded and in 1975 the present site of the Wangapeka Study and Retreat Centre near Nelson came up for sale and the Sphere Group bought it.

At that time there were no buildings, no roads and only three or four grand old beech trees surrounded by a lot of sun-burnt and wind-swept gorse, tutu, and knee-high bracken. With a great deal of enthusiasm and very little money, the initial road was put in, the main building (made partly from rammed earth) was started and 15,000 trees were planted.

Around this time a number of travellers returned to New Zealand after encountering the teachings of Buddhism in Asia. A small group of such students invited Lama Thubten Yeshe and Lama Thubten Zopa Rinpoche, based at a hilltop monastery near Kathmandu in Nepal, to visit New Zealand in 1974. The lamas made an immediate impact with their humour, quirky English and their red robes in the suburbs and on the beaches of Auckland.

Lama Yeshe encouraged the students to start a centre — the Dorje Chang Institute for Wisdom Culture. Since 1981, the Dorje Chang Institute has been home to three eminent Tibetan

Buddhist scholars: the late Geshe Thamchhu Sangpo, the late Geshe Kalsang Thapkey and Geshe Pal Tsering as well as many other resident and visiting teachers.

In 1978 another group of students purchased a property in Kaukapakapa, north of Auckland, and offered it to Lama Karma Thinley. The New Zealand Karma Kagyu Trust was established with the centre known as Karma Kagyu Thigsum Chokhorling. In the early 1980s, Lama Karma Samten arrived in New Zealand to live and teach at this centre in a beautiful rural hilltop setting. The centre and its facilities have continued to flourish under his guidance.

Still in the 1970s, other New Zealanders found their vocation in the Buddhist Sangha and took ordination as monks while in Asia. Bhikkhu Uppanno studied and was ordained in Thailand; Ham Wol took ordination vows in the Zen tradition in Korea.

When they returned to New Zealand these two monks provided a focus for the small but growing community of Asian Buddhists looking for pastoral support and New Zealanders eager to find out more about these traditions. The Auckland Theravada Buddhist Association was formed with represen-tatives of Sri Lankan, Burmese, Thai, Malaysian, Cambodian, Vietnamese, European and Laotian origins. The first informal meeting was held on 13 June 1980, and was attended by Phra

Mahasamai and Bhikkhu Uppanno and about forty other people. Phra Mahasamai, the abbot of the Sydney temple, happened to be visiting Auckland at the time. Not all the various communities were represented at the first meeting; the Laotians and Cambodians for instance had only just arrived in New Zealand as refugees through refugee camps in Thailand.

When Geshe Ngawang Dhargyey, from the Library of Tibetan Works and Archives in Dharamsala, first visited New Zealand in 1983, he was invited by one of the foremost Maori leaders, Dame Whina Cooper, to visit her tribal home in the north Hokianga. There Dame Whina told the oral history linking the lineage (or whakapapa) of their tribe to the Tibetan people.

Two years later Geshe Ngawang Dhargyey accepted an invitation by his students in Dunedin to return to New Zealand and establish a centre in that city. The Dhargyey Buddhist Centre was established and the Buddhists of Dunedin received the blessings of Rinpoche's teachings, until he passed away in August 1995. Since 1996, Jampa Thubten Tulku has been the resident spiritual guide at the centre.

During the 1980s several centres representing Theravada and Zen traditions as well as the Friends of the Western Buddhist Order (FWBO) were established in New Zealand. Significant among these are Bodhinyanarama, the forest retreat centre of the Theravada tradition in Stokes Valley near Wellington, and also the Auckland Buddhist Centre of the FWBO in Auckland. Towards the end of the decade, with the expansion of the Asian communities in New Zealand, many Buddhist groups from different Asian traditions were established.

In 1990, through the initiative of a Zen practitioner, Philippe Ercolano, the Auckland Pan-Buddhist Association was formed to represent the whole Auckland Buddhist community, fostering communication between traditions and acting as a voice for the Buddhist community liaising with public bodies and welfare agencies.

Two years later, during the Dalai Lama's first visit to New Zealand, he was joined by the ten senior Sangha of the Members of the Pan-Buddhist Association on the stage of the Aotea Centre in Auckland to celebrate Wesak, the holiest day of the Buddhist calendar. A multi-cultural children's choir sang songs especially composed for the day, the Chinese community chanted the *Heart Sutra* and the Tibetan centres made an extensive mandala offering. Over thirty ordained members of the Buddhist Sangha were present on this significant day for the growth of Buddhism in New Zealand.

During the Dalai Lama's second visit to New Zealand in 1996, he again toured the country, giving public talks in Wellington, Nelson, Christchurch, Dunedin and Auckland to more than 20,000 people. On a headland at Portobello, outside Dunedin, with its backdrop of green hills, blue skies and wind-swept seas, he blessed the relic stupa of Geshe Ngawang Dhargyey, whom he had appointed many years before as the first teacher of Westerners at the Library of Tibetan Works and Archives.

During his third visit in 2002, as well as giving his first formal Buddhist teaching in Nelson, the Dalai Lama will also open the International Buddhist Youth Congress attended by over two hundred delegates from twenty-five countries around the world.

Today almost every Buddhist tradition is represented in centres spread throughout New Zealand ranging from tiny rural retreats to large urban temples, from study groups to hospice services. The 2001 census revealed that Buddhism is the fastest growing religion in New Zealand.

Kirti Tsenshab Rinpoche, lineage holder of the Kalachakra, was asked last year what was the best place in the world to study and practise Dharma. His answer was immediate and forthright, 'New Zealand, particularly around Nelson'.

In January 2002, Thubten Kesang, a Tibetan residing in New Zealand, received the Queen's Service medal for Public Service. Since migrating to New Zealand, he has been active in promoting the cause of Tibet and providing humanitarian assistance to Tibetan refugees. He is a founding member of Friends of Tibet in New Zealand. Today, Friends of Tibet (NZ) has members throughout the country and is the largest network of Tibet support groups in New Zealand.

Glossary

Arhat   Literally 'foe destroyer'; a person who has destroyed his or her delusions and is freed from cyclic existence

ATC   Acronym for the Australia Tibet Council, which advocates human rights and justice for Tibet. ATC has a national office in Sydney and branches in every Australian state. Its web site is http://www.atc.org.au

Atisha   An eleventh-century Indian Buddhist monk, who revived Buddhism in Tibet and travelled to the southern hemisphere. Atisha, a prolific writer and renowned teacher, composed the *Lamp for the Path to Enlightenment*

bodhicitta   Literally 'Buddha mind'; the wish to practise compassion and altruism with the aim of relieving the sufferings of others, and bringing them to enlightenment

Bodhisattva   Someone whose spiritual practice is directed towards the achievement of enlightenment, for the sake of all beings; one who possesses the compassionate motivation of bodhicitta

Buddha   A fully enlightened being; the historical Buddha was Prince Siddhartha Gautama or the Buddha Shakyamuni, who lived in India in six hundred years BCE; the first of the Three Jewels of Refuge

Buddhadharma   The teachings of the Buddha

Chenrezig Known as *Avalokiteshvara* in Sanskrit; a male aspect of a deity symbolising compassion and altruism, Chenrezig is depicted with four or a thousand arms. The Dalai Lama is considered to be a living embodiment of Chenrezig in our time

chorten (*See* stupa)

compassion A close approximation of the Sanskrit term *karuna*; the altruistic wish to help free all beings from misery and suffering

cyclic existence The beginningless, recurring cycle of death and rebirth controlled by delusion and karma (*see* samsara)

Dalai Lama The temporal and spiritual leader of the Tibetan people, in Tibet and in exile. The present Dalai Lama is the fourteenth. The title Dalai Lama means Ocean of Wisdom. He is considered as the earthly manifestation of Chenrezig

deity A form used in meditation, visualisation or tantra. The deity represents an aspect of Buddhahood, or enlightened mind

deity yoga The practice of employing a deity in meditation, by visualising oneself as the deity, after receiving the initiation from a qualified teacher who holds the practice lineage

Dharma The spiritual teachings of the Buddha; the second of the Three Jewels of Refuge

Drol Kar   White Tara (*see* Tara)

Dzogchen   The 'Great Perfection' teachings of the Nyingma
School of Tibetan Buddhism

emptiness (*shunyata*)   The wisdom of realising the true
nature of all reality

enlightenment   The fully awakened, realised and omniscient
mind, pure and cleared of all obscurations. In Buddhism
every being is capable of evolving to such an enlightened
state by gradually transforming one's mind. Enlightenment
is the ultimate goal of Buddhist practice

Four Noble Truths   The Buddha's first teaching at Varanasi,
the Four Noble Truths is the foundation of Buddhist
thought and practice; the truths of suffering, the origin
of suffering, the cessation of suffering and the path to
the cessation of suffering

FPMT   Acronym for the Foundation for the Preservation of
the Mahayana Tradition, a world-wide organisation with
Buddhist meditation centres in cities and rural retreat
centres throughout Australia and New Zealand

Gelugpa   One of the four lineages of Tibetan Buddhism,
headed by the Dalai Lama and founded by Lama Tsong
Khapa in the fourteenth century

geshe   'Spiritual friend' in Tibetan; a spiritual teacher who
has completed formal intensive training and attained
the Geshe degree. The study primarily concentrates
on *Madhyamika*, the philosophy of the Middle Way;

Prajnaparamita, the perfection of wisdom; *Pramana*, logic
and epistemology; *Abidharma*, metaphysics; and *Vinaya*, the
monastic code of ethics

guru   (*See* lama)

Gyalwa Rinpoche   'The precious victorious one'; one of
the many titles by which Tibetans commonly refer to
the Dalai Lama

initiation (Tibetan: *wang*, Sanskrit: *abhisheka*)   An
empowerment, giving permission to the student to
perform practices associated with a meditational deity

Kagyu   One of the four lineages of Tibetan Buddhism,
originating from Marpa. His Holiness the seventeenth
Karmapa, exiled in India after a childhood in Tibet, is
head of this lineage

Kalachakra   The 'Wheel of Time' tantric system, which
includes instructions on medicine, astronomy, time, yoga
and physiology, encompassing the entire universe and the
path to enlightenment. It is frequently connected with the
promotion of world peace. (The Dalai Lama taught on
the Kalachakra in Sydney in 1996.)

karma   Literally meaning 'action' or 'deed' in Sanskrit. It is
the law of cause and effect, of actions having consequences
for oneself and others

Kundun   'Presence'; one of the titles Tibetans give to the
Dalai Lama

lama   Literally 'none higher'; Tibetan equivalent of the
Sanskrit term 'guru'; someone who can be trusted as a
teacher or spiritual friend and guide, and who can show
the pure path to enlightenment

Lama Tsong Khapa   A fourteenth-century teacher, writer and
one of Tibet's great philosophers. He founded the Gelugpa
tradition of Tibetan Buddhism. His work *The Great Treatise
on the Stages on the Path to Enlightenment (Lam Rim Chenmo)*,
has recently been published in English for the first time

Langri Tangpa   Born in Tibet in 1054, the year that Atisha
passed away, Langri Tangpa composed the poem *Eight
Verses of Thought Transformation*. This gave rise to the
practice, which has come to be known as *lojong* or
thought transformation (*see* lojong). The poem was taught
to the Dalai Lama as a small boy, and he has recited these
verses every day since as part of his personal practice. Also
known as *Eight Verses for Training the Mind or Mind Training
in Eight Verses*

lojong   Thought transformation, or training the mind;
comprises techniques to subdue the mind, to reduce
self-cherishing thoughts and to cherish others instead

Madhyamika   The most influential of the four major
philosophical schools of Indian Buddhism, based on the
Perfection of Wisdom Sutras of Shakyamuni Buddha and
founded by Nagarjuna. The term means the 'Middle Way'

Mahayana   The 'Great Vehicle'. This system of Buddhism
promotes reaching the goal of enlightenment, not just to

achieve enlightenment for oneself but in order to rescue all other beings from suffering. Mahayana Buddhism spread from India to China, Tibet, Japan, Korea, Mongolia, Bhutan and Vietnam

mandala   A three-dimensional or circular diagram representing the universe, or the dwelling of a deity

mantra   Literally 'that which protects the mind'; the recitation of syllables associated with a deity or practice

meditation   Becoming familiar with different states of mind using various techniques, such as breathing, visualisation, single-pointed concentration; a method to subdue, clear and train the mind

mind-possessor (Tibetan: *semchen*)   Any living being that has consciousness

mudra   Ritual hand gesture symbolising various activities and used with mantras to aid meditation

Nagarjuna   A second-century CE Indian scholar and writer, Nagarjuna propounded the Madhyamika or Middle-Way School of Emptiness

nirvana   The state of freedom from all suffering, delusions and karma, liberation from samsara

Nyingma   The 'ancient' tradition of Buddhism in Tibet, as distinguished from the second spread of teachings in the eleventh century; one of the four lineages of Tibetan Buddhism

Padmasambhava   Literally 'born of a lotus'; Indian tantric master and founder of the Nyingma school of Tibetan Buddhism; his influence is felt in all the four traditions of Buddhism

rebirth   The continuum of aspects of the mind after death that seek embodiment again according to the karma accumulated in past lives

refuge   The door to the Dharma path; a Buddhist takes refuge in the Three Jewels, having faith that they will lead one out of suffering and to enlightenment

rigpa   In the Dzogchen tradition, a state of intuitive and direct knowledge of the primordial clear light nature of the mind

Rinpoche   'Precious jewel', the title given to a precious teacher

sadhana   The practice and instructions given when taking on a commitment associated with a meditational deity

Sakya   One of the four lineages of Tibetan Buddhism; His Holiness Sakya Trizin is the current head of the school

shamatha (Tibetan: *shi-né*)   Calm abiding meditation

samsara   Cyclic existence, the wheel of continuous death and rebirth

Sangha   The Buddhist spiritual community, or ordained monks and nuns; the third of the Three Jewels of Refuge sentient being   Any living being with consciousness that is not free of gross and subtle ignorance

stupa   In Buddhist architecture, a dome-like structure symbolising qualities of enlightenment; often used to store texts, relics or the remains of spiritual teachers. Several stupas have been built in Australia and New Zealand including a replica of the Gyantse Stupa of Tibet near Bendigo, in country Victoria

shunyata   (*See* emptiness)

sutras   The teachings or scriptures of Buddha Shakyamuni

Tantra   The 'Diamond Vehicle'; the secret teachings of Mahayana Buddhism, used to progress rapidly on the path to enlightenment

Tara   A female deity who represents the energetic activity of all the Buddhas

thangka   A scroll painting, which depicts deities or symbols, such as the Wheel of Life, and is used for visualisation and meditation

Theravada   The dominant Hinayana school today; prevalent in India, Sri Lanka, Burma, Laos, Thailand and Cambodia and the West

Three Jewels   The Buddha, Dharma and Sangha; the object of refuge

Vajrayana   The 'Adamantine Vehicle' also known as Tantrayana or Mantrayana; the quickest path to enlightenment, for certain practitioners (*see* Tantra)

vipassana (Tibetan: *lhag tong*)   Insight meditation

wisdom   Different levels of insight into the nature of reality

Endnotes

Chapter one

1 Dalai Lama, *Training the Mind*, www.dalailama.com/htm/training.html
2 Dalai Lama, *Dimensions of Spirituality*: National Tennis Centre, Melbourne, 4 May 1992, www.wisdompubs.org/booklets/dimensions.html

Chapter two

1 Dalai Lama, from Nobel Peace Prize address, on the Government of Tibet in Exile's web site: www.tibet.com
2 Shantideva, from the Government of Tibet in Exile's web site: www.tibet.com
3 from web site: www.lontano.dk/scriptsa/kundun.html
4 Dalai Lama, *My Land and My People*, Potala, 1977, p. 233
5 *ibid.*, p. 216
6 *ibid.*, pp. 221–2
7 Dalai Lama, *Freedom in Exile: Autobiography of the Dalai Lama*, Harper Perennial, 1991, pp. 170–1
8 *ibid.*, p. 152
9 *ibid.*, p. 166
10 *My Land and My People, op. cit.*, p. 231
11 Dalai Lama, *Universal Responsibility and the Good Heart*, Library of Tibetan Works and Archives, 1977, p. 21
12 Glenn H. Mullin, *The Fourteen Dalai Lamas: A Sacred Legacy of Reincarnation*, Clear Light Publishers, Santa Fe, New Mexico, 2001, pp. 435–6
13 *ibid.*
14 *ibid.*, pp. 448–9
15 Charles Bell, *Portrait of a Dalai Lama: The Life and Times of the Great Thirteenth*, Wisdom Publications, Boston, 1987, p. 96; © The Canada Trust Company, Executor of the Estate of Sir Charles Bell, Deceased, 1987. Reprinted from *Portrait of a Dalai Lama* with permission of Wisdom Publications, 199 Elm Street, Somerville MA 02144, USA, www.wisdompubs.org
16 Mullin, *op. cit.*, p. 436
17 *ibid.*, p. 438
18 *ibid.*, p. 377

19   *ibid.*, p. 438
20   Hubert Decleer, 'Atisha's Journey to Tibet', in Donald Lopez (ed.) *Religions of Tibet in Practice*, Princeton University Press, 1997, pp. 171–2
21   Dalai Lama, *Training the Mind*, www.dalailama.com/htm/training.html
22   Pico Iyer, 'Over Tea with the Dalai Lama', published in *Shambhala Sun*, November 2001
23   *ibid.*
24   *Ordinary Mind* magazine, Kagyu Evam Buddhist Institute, Winter 1998
25   Dalai Lama, from a speech given in Prague, Czech Republic, 3 September 1997

Chapter four

1   Dalai Lama, *Training the Mind*, www.dalailama.com/htm/training.html
2   Chogyam Trungpa, *Training the Mind and Cultivating Loving-kindness*, Shambhala, 1993, p. xvii
3   *ibid.*
4   *ibid.*
5   *ibid.*
6   In 1997, the team of Geshe Sonam Rinchen and Ruth Sonam at the Library of Tibetan Works and Archives in Dharamsala, India, produced a rendition of *Atisha's Lamp for the Path to Enlightenment* which is both memorable and worth memorising (Snow Lion Publications, 1977).
7   *Training the Mind, op. cit.*

Chapter five

1   Marie Byles, *Journey into Burmese Silence*, Allen & Unwin, 1962, p. 140
2   *ibid.*, p. 28
3   *ibid.*, p. 166
4   *ibid.*, p. 28
5   Peter Kelly, *Buddha in a Bookshop. Harold Stewart and the Traditionalists: the story of Australian interest in Asian religions before 1960*, unpublished manuscript, quoted by explicit permission of the author
6   Elizabeth Bell, *Recollections of the Buddhist Society of Victoria*, self-published, 1999, permission to quote granted by the author
7   *Mandala Magazine*, September 1996
8   Sonam Rigzin, from an unpublished interview with Gabriel Lafitte, 1998

List of photographs

Text pages:

Clive Arrowsmith: portrait of the Dalai Lama, from the cover photograph, reproduced on the title page

Robert Beer: line drawings of the eight auspicious symbols, mandala and Dharma wheel reproduced throughout the design

Shane Marden: photograph taken in Tibet, of young Tibetan lighting butterlamps, page 80; photograph of the Norbulingka Palace in Tibet, page 41; photograph of stupa in Tibet, page 47

Than Nguy: photograph of the banner welcoming the Dalai Lama to the Quang Minh Temple in Melbourne, 1996, on page 195; photograph of the Dalai Lama and Sangha at Quang Minh Temple, page 212

Andy Weber: line drawing of Atisha reproduced on pages 78 and 167

William Yang: photograph of the Dalai Lama during the Kalachakra ceremony, Sydney, 1996, page 86; photograph of the Dalai Lama and Sangha, 1996, page 106

Colour pages:

Robert Beer: devotional paintings of Chenrezig, Shakyamuni Buddha and White Tara, opposite pages 59, 91 and 154

David Bell: portrait of Geshe Sonam Thargye, opposite page 186

Shane Marden: portrait of the Dalai Lama at Sarnath, January 2000, opposite page 58

Than Nguy: photographs of the Dalai Lama and Sangha at Quang Minh Temple in Melbourne, 1996, opposite page 187

Liz Thompson: photographs of the Dalai Lama in Australia, 1996, opposite page 186

Andy Weber: devotional painting of Atisha, opposite page 155

William Yang: photographs of the Dalai Lama during the Kalachakra ceremony in Sydney, Australia, 1996, opposite page 90

Acknowledgements

Clear Light Publications, Santa Fe, New Mexico: for quotes from *The Fourteen Dalai Lamas: A Sacred Legacy of Reincarnation*, Glenn H. Mullin, 2001; Clive Arrowsmith and the Office of Tibet, London: for permission to use the portrait of the Dalai Lama; Robert Beer: images of Shakyamuni Buddha, White Tara, Chenrezig and illustrations from *Encyclopaedia of Tibetan Symbols and Motifs*; David Bell: for the photograph of Geshe Sonam Thargye; Neil Cameron and Simon Harrison for the history of Buddhism in New Zealand, in Chapter Five; Robina Courtin and *Mandala Magazine*; the Dalai Lama in Australia 2002 Committee; FPMT Australia: for permission to use excerpts from the Dalai Lama's teachings in Australia, 1996; Library of Tibetan Work and Archives: for permission to quote from *Universal Responsibility and the Good Heart*; Shane Marden: for the portrait of the Dalai Lama and photographs taken in Tibet in 2000; Than Nguy (and Oscar Photography, Richmond, Victoria): for photographs of the Dalai Lama's visit to the Quang Minh Temple in Melbourne, 1996; the Office of His Holiness the Dalai Lama, Dharamsala, India: for permission to use copyrighted excerpts of teachings; Princeton University Press: for permission to quote from *Religions of Tibet in Practice*, Donald Lopez (ed.), 1997; Private Office of the Dalai Lama: for permission to quote from *My Land and My People*, *Freedom in Exile* and *Training the Mind*; QED Recording Services, Stephen Heliczer, London: for permission to use recorded excerpts from teachings given by the Dalai Lama in Australia in 1996; Nick Ribush; Geshe Sonam Rinchen and Ruth Sonam; *Shambhala Sun*: for permission to quote from 'Over Tea with the Dalai Lama', Pico Iyer, November 2001; Snow Lion Publications: for permission to use verses from *Atisha's Lamp for the Path to Enlightenment*; Geshe Sonam Thargye, Geelong; Liz Thompson: for photographs of the Dalai Lama in Australia, 1996; Andy Weber: for use of images of Atisha; Wisdom Publications, Boston, USA: for permission to quote from *Portrait of a Dalai Lama: the Life and Times of the Great Thirteenth*, Charles Bell, 1987(© The Canada Trust Company, Executor of the Estate of Sir Charles Bell, Deceased, 1987. Reprinted from *Portrait of a Dalai Lama* with permission of Wisdom Publications, 199 Elm Street, Somerville MA 02144, USA, www.wisdompubs.org); William Yang: for photographs of the Dalai Lama in Australia, 1996; the Lama Yeshe Wisdom Archive in Australia (Greg Sneddon and team).

Recommended reading

Buddhism and meditation

Chodron, Thubten. *Buddhism For Beginners*. Snow Lion Publications, 2001
Chodron, Thubten. *Open Heart, Clear Mind*. Snow Lion Publications, 1990
Chögyam Trungpa Rinpoche. *Meditation in Action*. Shambhala, 1996
Geshe Doga. *Inner Peace and Happiness, the Path to Freedom*. Lothian Books, 2002
Geshe Loden. *Meditations on the Path to Enlightenment*. Tushita Publications, 1996
Khema, Ayya. *Being Nobody, Going Nowhere, Meditations on the Buddhist Path*. Wisdom Publications, 1987
Lama Tsong Khapa. *The Great Treatise on the Path to Enlightenment (Lam Rim Chenmo)*. Snow Lion, 2000
Lama Yeshe. *Wisdom Energy*. Wisdom Publications, 1976, revised 2000
Mackenzie, Vicki. *Why Buddhism? Westerners in Search of Wisdom*. Allen and Unwin, 2000
McDonald, Kathleen. *How to Meditate*. Wisdom Publications, 1984
Powers, John. *Introduction to Tibetan Buddhism*. Snow Lion Publications, 1995
Sharples, Bob. *Meditation, Getting Started*. Lothian Books, 2002
Sogyal Rinpoche. *The Tibetan Book of Living and Dying*. Rider, 1993
Traleg Rinpoche. *The Essence of Buddhism, An Introduction to its Philosophy and Practice*. Shambhala, 2001
Ven. Gunaratana. *Mindfulness in Plain English*. Wisdom Publications, 1991
Wallace, Alan. *Tibetan Buddhism from the Ground Up, A Practical Approach to Modern Life*. Wisdom Publications, 1993

Some books by the Dalai Lama

Ancient Wisdom, Modern World: Ethics for a New Millennium. Little, Brown & Co., 1999
An Open Heart, Practising Compassion in Everyday Life. Hodder, 2001
Art of Happiness, a Handbook for Living. Hodder, 2000
Freedom in Exile. Abacus, 1998
Healing Anger, The Power of Patience from a Buddhist Perspective. Snow Lion Publications, 1997

Kindness, Clarity and Insight. Snow Lion Publications, 1998
The Meaning of Life, Buddhist Perspectives on Cause and Effect. Wisdom
    Publications, 2000
Path to Bliss, a Practical Guide to the Stages of Meditation. Snow Lion
    Publications, 1991
Policy of Kindness. Snow Lion Publications, 1993
The Transformed Mind: Reflections on Truth, Love and Happiness. Hodder, 2000
World of Tibetan Buddhism. Wisdom Publications, 1995

Further reading on the teachings

Dalai Lama, Hopkins. *Deity Yoga*. Snow Lion Publications, 1981
Dalai Lama. *Eight Verses for Training the Mind* (four cassette tapes). Snow
    Lion Publications, 1999
Geshe Sonam Rinchen. *Atisha's Lamp for the Path to Enlightenment*. Snow
    Lion Publications, 1997
Geshe Sonam Rinchen. *The Bodhisattva Vow*. Snow Lion Publications,
    2000
Geshe Sonam Rinchen. *Eight Verses for Training the Mind*. Snow Lion
    Publications, 2001
Geshe Tharchin. *Essence of Mahayana Lojong Practice*. Mahayana and Sutra,
    Tantra Press, 1998
Lama Yeshe. *Introduction to Tantra, the Transformation of Desire*. Wisdom
    Publications, 1987, revised 2001
Lama Zopa Rinpoche. *The Door to Satisfaction, the Heart Advice of a Tibetan
    Buddhist Master*. Wisdom Publications, 1994
Lama Zopa Rinpoche. *Transforming Problems into Happiness*. Wisdom
    Publications, 2001
Landaw, Weber. *Images of Enlightenment, Tibetan Art in Practice*. Snow Lion
    Publications, 1993
Ven. Gyatrul Rinpoche. *Generating the Deity*. Snow Lion Publications, 1996
Ven. Lobsang Gyatso. *The Four Noble Truths*. Snow Lion Publications, 1994
Wallace, Alan. *Buddhism with an Attitude*. Snow Lion Publications, 2001

Journals

Ordinary Mind, published by Kagyu Evam Buddhist Institute, Melbourne
Mandala Magazine, published by FPMT

Buddhist organisations

Australia

Australian Capital Territory

Chengawa Centre (FPMT)
PO Box 3017
Manuka ACT 2603
Ph: (02) 6295 0157

Diamond Way Buddhist Centre
11 Hakea Crescent
O'Connor ACT 2602
Ph: (02) 6257 7982

Dzogchen Community
Canberra
Ph: (02) 6248 6320

Rigpa (Canberra)
40 Mort Street
Braddon ACT 2612
Ph: (02) 6230 5093

Rongton Buddhist Training
College
14 Johnson Street
Narrabundah ACT 2603
Ph: (02) 6258 0452

Sakya Losal Choe-Dzong
The Tibetan Buddhist Society
of Canberra
Alderman Street
Evatt ACT 2617
Ph: (02) 6258 0452

New South Wales

Amitabha Centre
37 The Corso
Manly NSW 2095
Ph: (02) 9976 2363

Australian Institute of Tibetan
Healing Practices
Karana Place
Chatswood West NSW 2067
Ph: (02) 9411 2818

Australian Tibetan Buddhist
Centre
PO Box 1011
Murwillumbah NSW 2484
Ph: (02) 6679 5303

Blue Mountains Medicine
Buddha Dharma Group
834 Hawkesbury Road
Hawkesbury Heights NSW 2777
Ph: (02) 4754 3119

Blue Mountains Tibetan Healing
and Meditation Centre
PO Box 294
Blackheath NSW 2785
Ph: (02) 4787 6056

The Diamond Cutter Centre
Waterfall Arcade
Suite 10, 201 Mann Street
Gosford NSW 2250
Ph: (02) 4322 7088

Diamond Way Buddhist Centre
99 Gowrie Street
Newtown NSW 2042
Ph: (02) 9557 3275

Diamond Way Buddhist Group
5 Daley Street
Alstonville NSW 2477
Ph: (02) 6628 7002

Diamond Way Buddhist Group
18 Surf Road
Whale Beach NSW 2107
Ph: (02) 9974 4861

Drogmi Choe Ghar
PO Box 257
Pambula NSW 2549
Ph: (02) 6495 3423

Dzogchen Community
PO Box 14
Central Tilba NSW 2546
Ph: (02) 4473 7770

Dzogchen Community
Batemans Bay
    Ph: (02) 4471 8578
Katoomba Ph: (02) 4787 5706
Namgyalmar
    Ph: (02) 4473 7049
Northern NSW
    Ph: (02) 6684 5570
Richmond/Windsor
    Ph: (02) 4488 5213
Sydney Ph: (02) 9564 6306
Wollongong
    Ph: (02) 4268 2894

Institute of Buddhist Learning
    and Practice
15 Mettella Road
Toongabbie NSW 2146
Ph: (02) 9896 4613

Kadam Sherawa (FPMT)
Suite 2, Level 1, 190 Mann Street
Gosford NSW 2250
Ph: (02) 4324 8860

Karma Tashi Cho-Ling
PO Box 973
Bega NSW 2550
Ph: (02) 6496 7169

Karma Thekchen Choeling
PO Box 1579
Bondi Junction NSW 2022
Ph: (02) 9386 5929

Kyegu Buddhist Institute
3 Ivy Lane
Darlington NSW 2008
Ph: (02) 9699 0087

The Red Tara Group
7 McDonald Street
Balmain NSW 2050
Ph: (02) 9818 2650

Rigpa (Newcastle)
PO Box 397
Newcastle NSW 2300
Ph: (02) 4925 2770

Rigpa (Sydney)
Level 3, 822 George Street
Sydney NSW 2000
Ph: (02) 9211 5304

Sakya Dolma Choe Ling
7 Alexandra Avenue
Eastwood NSW 2122
Ph: (02) 9801 3209

Sakya Manjusri Centre
22 Hewison Street
Tighes Hill NSW 2297
Ph: (02) 4962 2492

Sakya Tharpa Ling
Tibetan Buddhist Institute and
    Meditation Centre
66 Evans Street
Rozelle NSW 2039
Ph: (02) 9555 9194

Sakya Trinley Ling
Katoomba NSW 2780
Ph: (02) 4782 3193

Tenzing Ling Retreat Centre
c/o Quaama Post Office
Quaama NSW 2550
Ph: (02) 6493 8344

Tibetan Buddhist Society
175 Dennison Road
Dulwich Hill NSW 2203
Ph: (02) 9569 0918

Vajra Ling Retreat Centre
PO Box 230
Uralla NSW 2358
Ph: (02) 6778 3700

**Vajrasattva Mountain Centre
(FPMT)**
155 Lurline Street
Katoomba NSW 2780
Ph: (02) 4782 1931

Vajrayana Institute (FPMT)
22 Linthorpe Street
Newtown NSW 2042
Ph: (02) 9550 2066

Yamantaka Buddhist Centre
31 Queens Street
Murwillumbah NSW 2484
Ph: (02) 6672 7923

Northern Territory

**Alice Springs Dzogchen
Community**
Ph: (08) 8953 2776

**Alice Springs Palyul Dharma
Group**
6 Lindsey Avenue
Old Eastside
Alice Springs NT 0870
Ph: (08) 8953 0808

**Institute of Buddhist Learning
and Practice**
Tsong Khapa Choe Tsog
133 Lee Point Road
Wagaman (Darwin) NT 0810
Ph: (08) 8927 6974

Queensland

Brisbane Study Groups
Ph: (07) 3396 3890

**Cairns Bodhi Citta Dzogchen
Centre**
Ph: (07) 4038 2482

**Chenrezig Institute for Wisdom
Culture (FPMT)**
Highlands Road
Eudlo Qld 4554
Ph: (07) 5445 0077

**Chenrezig Nuns Community
(FPMT)**
PO Box 41
Eudlo Qld 4554
Ph: (07) 5445 0077

Chogye Padma Choe Dzong
PO Box 11
Torquay Qld 4655
Ph: (07) 4125 7127

**Cittamani Hospice Service
(FPMT)**
PO Box 324
Palmwoods Qld 4555
Ph: (07) 5445 0822

**Dzogchen Community
Queensland**
Ph: (07) 3369 8632

Institute of Buddhist Learning
and Practice
Kunga Choling Dharma Centre
18 Byrne Street
Windsor Qld 4030
Ph: (07) 3357 3958

Karuna Hospice Service
(FPMT)
PO Box 2020
Windsor Qld 4030
Ph: (07) 3857 8555

Langri Tangpa Centre (FPMT)
51 Enoggera Road
Newmarket (Brisbane) Qld 4051
Ph: (07) 3356 9523

Liberation Prison Project
(FPMT)
PO Box 41
Eudlo Qld 4554
Ph: mob. 0412 589 842

Padma Buddhist Centre
Maryborough Qld 4650
Ph: (07) 4122 4362 or
(07) 4121 6910

Rigpa Brisbane
8 Hamley Street
Wooloowin Qld 4030
Ph: (07) 3262 6256

Rigsum Gonpo Tibetan
Buddhist Centre (FPMT)
25 Kiernan Street
Cairns North Qld 4870
Ph: (07) 4053 2915

Tibetan Buddhist Centre for
the Liberation from Samsara
(FPMT)
19 Alfred Street
Gympie Qld 4570
Ph: (07) 5483 8131

Tibetan Buddhist Healing
Practices
18 Mynah Crescent
Condon (Townsville) Qld 4815
Ph: (07) 4723 8849

Tsechen Buddhist Centre
PO Box 1465
Toowong (Brisbane) Qld 4066
Ph: (07) 3856 1034

Tibetan Buddhist Society
Queensland
10 Lomond Terrace
East Brisbane Qld 4169
Ph: (07) 3391 5723

South Australia
Buddha House (FPMT)
3 Nelson Street
Fullarton SA 5063
Ph: (08) 8379 9153

De-Tong Ling Retreat Centre
(FPMT)
RSD 418
via Kingscote SA 5223
(Kangaroo Island)
Ph: (08) 8559 3276

Diamond Way Buddhist Group
PO Box 1204
Mount Barker SA 5251
Ph: (08) 8391 3361

Dzogchen Community Adelaide
Ph: (08) 8357 7400

Gyuto House
Riverside Drive
Second Valley (Adelaide) SA 5204
Ph: (08) 8598 4136

Palden Sakya Centre
Norwood SA 5067
Ph: (08) 8361 3151

Rigpa
PO Box 10440
Gouger Street
Adelaide SA 5000
Ph: (08) 8411 6113

Rongton Buddhist Study Group
PO Box 191
Brompton SA 5007
Ph: (08) 8346 3206

Sakya Yigah Choe Ling
PO Box 297
Whyalla SA 5600

**South Australian Meditation
Centre**
PO Box 481
North Adelaide SA 5006
Ph: (08) 8388 6619

**South Australian Meditation
Centre**
2 Beulah Road
Norwood SA
Ph: (08) 8370 9701

Tasmania

**Chag-Tong Chen-Tong Centre
(FPMT)**
Hobart Tas. 7000
Ph: (03) 6267 9203

Dorje Ling Retreat Centre
(formerly Illusion Farm)
PO Box 132
Sheffield Tas. 7306
Ph: (03) 6363 5178

Karma Kagyu Buddhist Group
Ph: mob. 0417 551 990

Sukhavati Forest Retreat
PO Box 49
Meander Tas. 7304
Ph: (03) 6369 5275

Tashi Chöling Buddhist Centre
71 Liverpool Street
Hobart Tas. 7000
Ph: (03) 6234 4223

Victoria

Atisha Centre (FPMT)
RMB 1530
Eaglehawk (Bendigo) Vic. 3556
Ph: (03) 5446 3336

Chogye Jamchen Choe Dzong
(Jamchen Buddhist Centre)
19 Austin Street
Balwyn Vic. 3103
Ph: (03) 9817 3577 or
     (03) 9898 6977

Drol Kar Buddhist Centre
160 Portarlington Road
Newcomb (Geelong) Vic. 3219
Ph: (03) 5248 2727

**Dromtonpa Study Group
(FPMT)**
PO Box 172
Daylesford Vic. 3460
Ph: (03) 5348 2866

Dzogchen Community
Geelong
Ph: (03) 5261 3513
Melbourne
Ph: (03) 9481 5414

Kagyu Evam Buddhist Institute
673–691 Lygon Street
North Carlton Vic. 3054
Ph: (03) 9387 0422

**Maitripa Contemplative
Centre**
(Kagyu Evam Meditation Retreat)
528 Myers Creek Road
Healesville Vic. 3777

Mandala Books (FPMT)
PO Box 8111
Camberwell North Vic. 3124
Ph: (03) 9882 2484

Mandala Magazine (FPMT)
Ph: (03) 9437 1013

Melbourne Sakya Centre
(Choekhor Lhunpo)
PO Box 183
South Yarra Vic. 3141
Ph: (03) 9867 7291

Odiyana Buddhist Centre
14 Auburn Grove
Hawthorn East Vic. 3123
Ph: (03) 9813 2431

Odiyana Retreat Longchen
Osel Ling
Ameys Track
North Foster (South Gippsland)
Vic. 3960
Ph: mob. 0418 455 588

Prajna Maitri/Lama Yeshe Wisdom
Archive in Australia (FPMT)
Ph: (03) 9505 9211

Rigpa
Unit 8A, 205–207 Johnson Street
Fitzroy Vic. 3056
Ph: (03) 9417 4488

Serlingpa Centre
83 Mathiesons Road
Eagle Point Vic. 3878
Ph: (03) 5156 7240

Shen Phen Ling Albury–
Wodonga Study Group
(FPMT)
PO Box 178
Wodonga Vic. 3690
Ph: (02) 6033 2355

The Stupa of Universal
Compassion (FPMT)
(Tse-Chen Cho-Khor Ling Stupa)
Ph: (03) 5442 2866

Tara Institute (FPMT)
3 Mavis Avenue
East Brighton Vic. 3187
Ph: (03) 9596 8900

Thubten Shedrup Ling
Monastery (FPMT)
RMB 1530
Eaglehawk (Bendigo) Vic. 3556

Tibetan Buddhist Society
1425 Mickleham Road
Yuroke Vic. 3063
Ph: (03) 9333 1770

Tibetan Buddhist Society
Beaumaris Buddhist Meditation
Centre
27 Haywood Street
Beaumaris Vic. 3193
Ph: (03) 9589 1838

Western Australia

Diamond Way
PO Box 219
Melville WA 6956
Ph: (08) 9330 5864

Hayagriva Buddhist Centre
(FPMT)
64 Banksia Terrace
Kensington WA 6151
Ph: (08) 9367 4817

Hospice of Mother Tara
(FPMT)
Unit 3, 2B Victoria Street
Bunbury WA 6230
Ph: (08) 9791 9798

Origin Centre
Balingup WA 6253
Ph: (08) 9764 1109

Rigpa
89 Lakelands Village
Wanneroo WA 6065
Ph: (08) 9306 9486

Tashi Choeling
23 Goneril Way
Coolbellup WA 6163
Ph: (08) 9337 7669

Tibetan Buddhist Society
7 Alvan Street
Mt Lawley WA 6050
Ph: (08) 9370 1795

New Zealand

Auckland

Amitabha Hospice Service (FPMT)
6 Lyttleton Crescent
Forrest Hill (Auckland)
Ph: (09) 410 1431

Dalai Lama Trust New Zealand
PO Box 5429
Wellesly Street
Auckland
Ph: (09) 483 7275

Dorje Chang Institute (FPMT)
56 Powell Street
Avondale (Auckland)
Ph: (09) 828 3333

Karma Kagyu Trust
66 Bodhisattva Road
Kaukapakapa (Auckland)
Ph: (09) 420 5428

Tho Sam Dhargyey Ling
29 Princes Street
Auckland
Ph: (09) 377 2686

Trashi Gomang Buddhist Centre
31 Macintyre Road
Mangere Bridge (Auckland)
Ph: (09) 636 9810

Christchurch

Karma Thigsum Choeling
37 Warden Street
Christchurch
Ph: (03) 386 0085

Thubten Shenphen Dhargyey Ling
Cranmer Centre
Montral Street
Christchurch
Ph: (03) 379 2084

Other New Zealand centres

Chandrakirti Buddhist Centre (FPMT)
Sunrise Valley Road
Upper Moutere, Nelson
Ph: (03) 543 2015

Jam Tse Dhargyey Ling
159 Parakiore Road
Kamo, Whangarei
Ph: (09) 435 4444

Mahamudra Centre (FPMT)
RD4 Colville
Coromandel
Ph: (07) 866 6851

Phuntsok Choeling
PO Box 671
Napier
Ph: (06) 834 0050

**Thubten Shadrub Dhargyey
    Ling**
22 Royal Terrace
Dunedin
Ph: (03) 477 8374

Trashi Ge Phel Ling
20 Carlton Street
Melrose, Wellington
Ph: (04) 972 2472

Yangtse Rinpoche Foundation
22 Royal Terrace
Dunedin
Ph: (03) 455 7503

Other organisations

**The Australia Tibet Council
    (ATC)**
National Office
PO Box 1236
Potts Point NSW 2011
Ph: (02) 9807 1558

The ATC has branches in all States. Please contact the national office of the ATC for current details.

Tibetan Community of Australia
PO Box 146
Kew East Vic. 3102
Ph. (03) 9859 7106

Tibetan Friendship Group (TFG)
PO Box 39
Gordon NSW 2072
Ph: (02) 9918 4606

The TFG has been fundraising and finding sponsors for Tibetan refugee children for more than forty years.

Tibet Information Office
The office of the Dalai Lama's official representative.

In Australia, contact Chope Paljor Tsering on (02) 6285 4046; in New Zealand, contact Thubten Kesang on (09) 9483 7275

Tibet Welfare Group (TWG)
PO Box 618
Hawthorn Vic. 3122
Ph: (03) 9443 0707

The TWG raises funds for developmental aid projects in Tibetan communities in exile and in Tibet.

Index

A

Aborigines 213–15
afflictive emotions 91, 115,
    117–18, 122–4, 140,155
altruism 99–100, 118, 164
anger 118, 120, 124, 158
Arhat 99
Atisha 29, 30, 39, 40, 68
    life story 72–9
    teachings 162–7
Australian centres and teachers
    196–215
    Friends of the Western
        Buddhist Order 198
    Rigpa 205
    Dzogchen 206–7
    Sakya 207–8
    Nyingma 205–7
    Kagyu 205
    Gelugpa 199–204, 208
    FPMT 199–202
awakening 4–5, 17, 23, 80, 97–8,
    121, 138

B

Bell, Elizabeth 197
Buddha 7, 17, 30, 86, 132, 169
    refuge 95–9
    teachings 138–9
Buddhist Society of New South
    Wales 196
Buddhist Society of Victoria 196
Byles, Marie 189–91

C

Chenrezig 9, 42, 47, 177, 179,
    196

initiation 180–3
Communist Party (China) 54, 56
compassion 9, 33–4, 42, 74, 148,
    152–3, 180–4
confidence 6, 30

D

Dalai Lama
    Fourteenth Dalai Lama 40–60
        Asia 44
        Australia 211
        awards 45
        childhood 40
        China 54
        democracy 44, 58
        enthronement 41
        environmentalism 46
        Europe 43
        exile 43, 56
        government in exile 44
        India 43, 55
        interfaith 48
        Kundun 12, 53
        Nobel Peace Prize 45
        refugees 44, 59
        teachings 85–113
        United States of America 43
    Thirteenth Dalai Lama 39,
        61–72
        Bell, Charles 67
        British, in India 62, 63–6
        Curzon, Lord 68
        Empress of China 64
        Manchu Emperor 62
        Minto, Lord 68
        Queen Victoria 63
        Russia 67

Dharamsala   199
Dharma   20, 30, 86, 88, 91, 96,
    122, 155, 168
  taking refuge in   100–1
dissatisfaction   24, 85, 91, 107–10,
    137–46, 151

E
ego   25–7, 120, 142–4
emotions   (see afflictive emotions)
empowerment   (see initiation)
emptiness   (see shunyata)
enlightenment   (see awakening)

F
faith   87–8, 119
Four Noble Truths   107, 137,
    138–46

G
Gandhi, Mahatma   80–2

H
habit   18, 22, 28, 142, 170
happiness   2, 23, 92–5, 144
hospices   201–2

I
ignorance   111–15
Initiation   31, 102–3, 177–80

J
jealousy   160

K
Kalachakra   85, 87
karma   20, 21, 121, 123, 125

L
Lamas   1, 29, 59
Langri Tangpa   147, 148

Lhasa   41, 52
lineage   30, 103–5
lojong   27, 147–62

M
Mahayana   50, 100, 103–4, 172,
    177, 198, 200
mantra   177, 180, 182, 185
meditation   4, 18–20, 26, 97,
    143
mind   126–7, 144
mind training   (see lojong)
mindfulness   19

N
Nagarjuna   127, 128, 129
Nehru, Jawaharlal   57
Nepal   199
New Zealand centres and teachers
    215–21
nirvana   23
non-violence   80, 82, 171

P
patience   26, 159
purification   170

R
rebirth   21–3, 125, 126, 179
refuge   86, 95, 98, 100, 165,
    169
  refuge prayer   168
relaxation   3–4, 176

S
samsara   23, 109, 181
Sangha   20, 30, 96, 98, 100, 168
Shakyamuni   (see Buddha)
shunyata   8, 75, 111–14, 127–30,
    172–3
suffering   (see dissatisfaction)

T
Tara   (*see* White Tara)
Theravadan centres   198
Three Jewels   20, 30, 96, 98, 184
   taking refuge in   165
Tibet   1, 39–47, 50–9, 62–70, 73,
      76, 77, 79, 81, 82, 148

V
Vietnam War   198

W
welfare work   209
wisdom   (*see* shunyata)
White Tara   9, 10, 177, 179
   initiation   183–5

Z
Zen Buddhist Society   198

Care of this book

Please treat this book with care and respect as it contains
Buddhist teachings and images.

Dedication

This book is dedicated to the long life of His Holiness the
Dalai Lama, the Tibetan people, and to all beings, at all times
and everywhere. May all beings have peace and happiness.